Environmental Impact Assessment

Available techniques, emerging trends

ENVIRONMENTAL IMPACT ASSESSMENT

AVAILABLE TECHNIQUES, EMERGING TRENDS

By

S.A. Abbasi

Ph.D., DSc, FIE, PE
Senior Professor & Director
Centre for Pollution Control & Energy Technology
Pondicherry University
Pondicherry - 605 014
(India)

&

D.S. Arya

ME, Ph.D.
Senior Lecturer
Dept. of Hydrology
University of Roorkee
Roorkee - 247 667 (India)

DISCOVERY PUBLISHING HOUSE PVT. LTD.

NEW DELHI-110 002

Published by:
Tilak Wasan

DISCOVERY PUBLISHING HOUSE PVT. LTD.
4383/4B, Ansari Road, Darya Ganj
New Delhi-110 002 (India)
Phone : +91-11-23279245, 23253475, 43596065
E-mail : discoverypublishinghouse@gmail.com
sales@discoverypublishinggroup.com
web : www.discoverypublishinggroup.com

***First Edition:* 2000**

***Reprinted:* 2020**

ISBN: 978-81-7141-554-0

Environmental Impact Assessment:
Available Techniques, Emerging Trends

Printed at:
Infinity Imaging Systems
Delhi

DEDICATED TO

Professor Shamsul-Haq Alvi

University of Bahrain

and

Professor Tahir Husain

University of Newfoundland

Prof S. A. Abbasi

Smt Lila and Shri Ved Prakash Bharti

Dr. D. S. Arya

FOREWORD

Any developmental activity aimed at benefiting mankind shall serve its purpose only if it is compatible with the environment. As this realization downed upon the world during the late 1960s, the science of environmental impact assessment began to emerge.

Environmental impact assessment aims at determining the positive and negative impacts a developmental activity shall have on the environment. It then draws up the balance sheet to tell the regulatory agencies whether the project shall cause net benefit or net loss after taking into account the costs of environmental impacts besides all other costs and benefits.

But quantifying environmental impacts is an exceedingly vexing problem. How to put a Rupee value to a species of a bird going extinct due to a large dam? How to measure the loss if a thermal power plant would tarnish the walls of an ancient temple?

Then, again, very major complexities are faced in deciding upon what aspects of environment to be assessed in a given context. Environment is an all-encompassing sphere with literally millions of living organisms involved besides humans. Then we have rivers, wells, lakes; we have soils of bewildering verity; we have air and its pollution; we have numerous structures of historical or artistic value. We have problems of human population, of human aspirations, of complex interplay of interests and counter-interests. Any exercise in environmental impact assessment must consider *all* the important [illegible]nts. But how to chose what is important from this mind-boggling [illegible] of parameters? We can't simply study *all* aspects; it will be more costly than the developmental project itself.

The authors of this book have been grappling with these problems and contributing to their solutions since a long while. Dr D.S. Arya happens to be one among a handful of experts whose ME, PhD, and post-doctoral work has all focussed on methodologies of environmental impact assessment. Prof Abbasi has been associated with this field right from its inception. The authors thus have a combined experience of over 30 man-years in this field. The knowledge and the perspectives they have gained over these years have been distilled into this book.

I hope the book shall be useful to academics, industrial professionals, and students.

Dr. V.T.Patil,
Vice Chancellor,
Pondicherry University, Pondicherry

PREFACE

Environmental impact assessment emerged as a major branch of environmental engineering during the 1970s. It was the period in which one region of the world after another noticed the rising spectre of environmental pollution. One after another the governments of various countries began insisting on environmental impact assessment as a precondition for licencing new projects.

The requirement to do EIA generated need for appropriate methodologies. The initial methodologies - such as panel discussions and checklists - were *qualitative* and *ad-hoc*. In 1971 Leopold and coworkers introduced what is popularly known as *Leopold Matrix* which is the first ever methodology presented for *quantitative* EIA. In subsequent years Leopold Matrix was improved upon, and other methodologies such as impact network analysis were introduced.

This brief recapitulation of the history of EIA would indicate how recent this science is!

As more and more EIAs were done across the world the shortcomings of the available methodologies were seen more and more clearly. Attempts to overcome these inadequacies have led to newer methodologies but only a very few of these have been able to stand the test of field trials; the rest have began and ended their life span in the pages of reports or papers which had announced them.

What are the EIA methodologies reported thus far? What are their virtues and shortcomings? What are the requirements of an *ideal methodology* and how does one proceed towards approximating that ideal? The present book deals with these questions. It begins with an overview of the existing EIA methodologies. The ones commonly used as well as the ones less-tried or untried, are reviewed. The book simultaneously identifies the strenths and the weaknesses of these methodologies and focuses on the attributes desired to achieve *comprehensiveness* in EIA at the *least cost* and in the *shortest possible time*. It then presents three new methodologies - which together form a system or a logical sequence - and demonstrates their applicability with reference to a real-life study area.

We shall look forward to receiving your valuable comments so that we may improve upon this little effort in the next editions of the book.

S.A.Abbasi
D.S.Arya

CONTENTS

1

GENERAL INTRODUCTION

EIA (Environmental Impact Assessment) is one of the more recently emerged branches of environmental engineering but it has taken an increasingly dominant role over the past few years. All over the world governments have made it mandatory that all developmental activities must be preceded by EIA; as such the fate of new projects is increasingly being decided by the results of EIA rather than the conventional benefit cost criteria. There are increasing instances of such projects not getting clearance which had high potential of profit but which were likely to cause serious harm to the environment.

Whereas myriad techniques and tools are available to assess the impact of one or other environmental parameter - for example mercury on fish or sulfur dioxide on a crop - very few methods exist for *integrating* the numerous such impacts so as to resolve the EIA studies to a final score in terms of a single set of digits. Such summation is essential in order to find out how beneficial impacts weigh against harmful ones; it is also essential if one has to choose between alternative projects or alternative ways of implementing a given type of project.

There is also, as yet, no proven methodology to enable, objectively, the identification of key parameters out of a large number one normally encounters during any EIA. As EIA is a costly and time consuming exercise it is necessary to separate the man from the boys - so to speak - in order to optimize costs and efforts. A methodology which could help us in arranging the influencing parameters in the order of their importance to generate a hierarchical structure is also lacking. Such a methodology would give us an understanding of the nature, directions and importance of the influence of various parameters, thereby enabling us to determine which ones play a dominant role and which ones are merely peripheral.

AN OVERVIEW OF COMMON METHODOLOGIES OF COMPOSITE EIA

The methodologies of environmental impact assessment commonly used are :

i) Ad-hoc approaches
ii) Checklist
iii) Overlays
iv) Matrices
v) Impact tree analysis
vi) Indices
vii) Delphi

Of these, the most extensively used methodalogy for impact summation in EIA across the world is the 'matrix' approach in which project actions and their impacts are listed as rows and columns of table headings. The nature (positive or negative) and magnitude of impact are given as matrix elements. When scores of individual matrix 'cells' are summed it leads to a net score. One or the other variants of this approach - the Leopold Matrix, Betalle Environmental Evaluation System, Fisher & Davies Matrix, being well known examples - are in common use.

SHORTCOMINGS OF THE EXISTING METHODOLOGIES

The existing methodologies have some advantages; they also suffer from major shortcomings. Attempts to overcome these shortcomings has led to the search of newer techniques and development of newer methods. These aspects are reviewed in detail. This review reveals that:

i) thus far most of the 'emerging' methodologies have not been able to stand the test of extensive field trials; in other words these methodologies are largely confined to paper;

ii) the reasons for this, essentially, are that most of the newer methodologies either require information on the precise nature of inter-parameter relationships (which simply are not available in most cases), or they are computationally or experimentally too cumbersome (and/or unwieldy or costly) to be of much practical utility;

iii) no single *system* of methodologies is available which enables all the three stages of EIA to be accomplished viz a) identification of parameters to be studied b) assessment of their trends and c) impact summation.

We have made attempts to develop methodologies to overcome some of the abovementioned shortcomings. A system of three methodologies has been developed which may enable all the three stages of EIA to be accomplished. It includes :

i) a formulation and software package INTRA for the identification of key parameters out of a large number one invariably encounters during any EIA. It also helps us in arranging the influencing parameters in the order of their importance to generate a hierarchical structure. We hope that such a methodology would help us in understanding the nature, directions and importance of the influence of various parameters enabling us to determine which ones play a dominant role and which ones are merely peripheral;

ii) a designer software package incorporating the tests and tools needed to process basic data pertaining to typical EIA.

iii) a methodology and software package to integrate the individual environmental impacts for generating net impact scores. This system also enables generation of scenarios and deciding which of the scenarios are environmentally viable.

The application of these on a real-life situation has then been demonstrated.

2

EIA METHODOLOGIES CURRENTLY IN USE

2.1 INTRODUCTION

All activities cause an impact on environment. Bigger the activity stronger, the impact. In ecosystems not influenced by human perturbations, such activities even out and the impacts get assimilated or get fitted into the natural scheme of things. But human-induced developmental activities, especially big projects, have the potentiality to cause impacts which may disturb ecological balance beyond the ecosystem's assimilative capacity. Till a few decades ago we had not realised that the furious pace of development may cause such environmental impacts which may harm the natural resource base and cause losses - not only ecological but consequent monetary losses as well - in the long run. Towards the end of the sixth decade this realisation began to dawn upon mankind and the science of environmental impact assessment (EIA) began to taken shape.

2.2 CONCEPT OF ENVIRONMENTAL IMPACT ASSESSMENT - AN OVERVIEW

The major purpose of all environmental policies is to ensure that environmental quality is fully considered when taking the decisions on whether to take a developmental project or not. The vehicle used to accomplish this is environmental impact assessment whose specific objective is to provide a means for giving environmental quality a careful and appropriate consideration in the planning and decision-making process. EIA can be used for three principal functions :

i) as a decision-making instrument, to decide whether an envisaged project is acceptable from the point of view of its costs;
ii) as decision-making instrument to choose between different ways of doing a project or locations in which it can be done; and
iii) as a planning tool, to minimize adverse impacts that may be caused by the project.

By definition an environmental impact is any alteration of environmental conditions, adverse or beneficial, caused or induced by an action or set of actions. The attention given to environmental conditions as referred to here, will vary according to the nature, scale, and location of the proposed action (or actions). It is important that the impacts of a proposed action (project) on the quality of the of the physical environment be objectively weighed with the impacts on the social, aesthetic, and economic environments, over both the short and the long run.

Overall, the environmental impact assessment process provides a formalized procedure for generating, collecting, analysing and documenting information on all aspects of present status and possible impacts of a given project. In other words 'impact assessment' is an objective analysis conducted to identify and measure the likely economic, social, aesthetic, and environmental effects of the proposed action (activity or project) and the various reasonable alternatives. This requires the identification, measurement, and aggregation of the impacts to provide a total assessment.

The *identification* of impacts requires one to first describe and understand the conditions of the environment prior to the activity. There may be significant differences in impacts for a given activity in different areas. Geographical location is, therefore, one of the factors that affects the relative importance of an impact. For example, the impact of a specific project on water quality in an area with abundant water supplies would differ significantly from the impact of the same project on an area with scarce water resources. Furthermore, the timing and duration of each significant impact is to be determined. Impacts are to be described to establish their effect on the immediate project area, within the adjacent area and the community (or region) as a whole. The timing of impacts should be identified to establish whether they are likely to occur during construction, shortly after the project is completed, or at some later time. The nature of impacts should be identified to establish whether they are reversible or irreversible, and duration to establish whether they are short-term or long-term.

The *measurement* of impacts is the next logical step in the impact assessment process. Ideally, all impacts should be translatable into common units. However, this is not possible because of the difficulty of defining several impacts (such as on income, on noise quality, and on rare or endangered species) in common units. Another difficulty is that in some cases the quantification of impacts may be beyond the state-of-the-art. Therefore, one is generally faced with use of both quantitative and qualitative measurement techniques. In the latter case, it may be necessary to rely on expert judgment to answer the question of how the various dimensions of the environment are affected.

The final step involves the *aggregation* of project impacts into an overall assessment of the project's effects. One problem at this point is how to aggregate among the different measured impacts (quantitative and qualitative) to arrive at a single measure, or score, for project impact. This would involve expressing the various impact measures in common units or establishing a weighting-of-importance scheme to generate this single measure. This desire is perhaps more ideal than realistic or practical. However, eventhough subjective and rather less-than-comprehensive in nature, schemes do exist for accomplishing this objective. In many cases, however, it may suffice to present the measurement of the impacts in simple terms relative to each impact area such as air quality, community economy, energy, environmental quality, fish and wildlife resources, historical preservation, land use, noise quality, solid waste, transportation, and water quality.

2.3 COMMONLY USED METHODOLOGIES

2.3.1 Ad-hoc methods

Ad-hoc methods provide qualitative assessment of the total impact while suggesting the broad areas of possible impacts and the general nature of these possible impacts. For example, impacts on plant and animal life might be stated as minimal but adverse, whereas the impacts on the regional economy might be stated as significant and extremely beneficial. These statements are qualitative and could be based on subjective or intuitive assessments, or could be qualitative interpretations of quantitative results. The simplest approach to evaluating the total impact of a project by this method would be to consider each environmental area and identify the nature of the impact upon it, such as no effect, problematic, short-term or long-term and reversible or irreversible.

This method, as the name suggests, is *ad-hoc* with little quantitatification or precision. Nevertheless the method is ueful when discussing impacts of very large systems such asHimalayans echology on flooding in plains downstream (CSE, 1990), acid rain on global environment (Cresser & Edwards, 1987), degradation of Indian lands (Gadgil, 1993), or aquatic weeds on water resources (Abbasi & Nipaney, 1993). It can also become effective pre-EIA excercise in some situations, (Abbasi, etal. 1995).

Checklists

The use of *impact checklists* provides a method of combining a list of potential impact areas that need to be considered in the environmental impact assessment process with an assessment - often qualitative - of the individual impacts. This approach has been followed by a number of public agencies since it ensures that a prescribed list of areas is considered in the assessment process. A recent example of an elaborate checklist is the one developed for assessment environmental impact of water resources projects (Abbasi, 1991; Abbasi & Bhatia, 1993).

Checklists may be provided to facilitate rapid assessment of environmental impacts, qualitatively. Environmental protection authorities may provide such checklists for specific type of projects to ensure all important items are given due consideration. For example, there may be a specific checklist for water resources development projects, another for petrochemical industries, another for oil terminals and so on. In India, Central Governments

Department of Environment, Forests & Wildlife has prepared extensive-checklists for a variety of developmental activities which it uses in impact assessment as well as post-project environmental monitoring.

Checklists do not provide for the establishment of direct cause-effect links to the various project activities and, generally, does not include an overall interpretation of the collective environmental impacts.

Items included in a checklist are often of a broad nature and the likely impacts are stated qualitatively as beneficial or adverse, reversible or irreversible, short-term or long-term local or widespread.

The main advantage of a checklist is that it promotes thinking about the array of impacts in a systematic way and allows concise summarization of effects. Disadvantages stem from the fact that checklists may be too general or incomplete; they do not illustrate interactions between effects; the same effect may be registered in several places under headings that overlap in content (double counting); and the number of categories to be reviewed can be immense, thus distracting attention from the more significant impacts. The identification of effects being qualitative and subjective (for example, *water quality will be adversely affected*), as such these predictions cannot be tested with accuracy and precision. Furthermore, no statements of likelihood of occurrence are being made. Because of the subjective nature of estimates, checklists are often not filled out identically by different investigators. It gives the descriptive evaluation of the impacts (Mongkol, 1982), but it is not always adequate for carrying out a comprehensive environmental assessment (Heer and Hagerty, 1977).

Expert opinion

If the number of experts is large and properly chosen, the above errors can be minimised. However the opinion polls or surveys tend to drown minority opinions, however much perceptive they may be. Further, the respondents get no opportunity to reconsider their views.

Opinion polls or surveys are widely used in social forecasting, and impact analysis (Agrawal. , 1995; Kalshian, 1995). There it is a matter of finding out people's ideas, perceptions and attitudes about societal change, and surveys become a useful tool.

Panels

In this method, a group of experts interacts across a table. Panels are suitable when the subject under consideration requires discussion and analysis. The process is very valuables for identification of important problems, for initial assessments, and for policy analysis and evaluation. Multidisciplinary problems are taken care of by a suitable choice of the panelists. For example the possible impacts of a ecology curriculam was assessed through panel approach (Abbasi etal,1995)

Panels, however, suffer from the following major disadvantages:

i) views not in line with majority opinion may get eliminated, due to the pressuretoobtain a consensus;
ii) the opinions of the most vociferous speakers, or the person with highest bureocratic status will be given disproportionate representation;
iii) in the same way, the views of persons less vocal or junior in status may not be heard; and
iv) many people are afraid of abandoning views expressed by them earlier, even after realising their flaws, due to fear of losing face.

Brainstorming

This is a modified panel approach, and one which is very suitable for exploring out-of-the way ideas. The meetings are held in an uninhibited environment, with imagination being given free rein.

When properly conducted, brainstorming sessions may yield a wealth of new ideas, which can later be assessed for feasibility and constraints. Although the great majority of ideas will be promptly culled out, worthwhile ideas might emerge. The technique has the great advantage of stimulating imagination and creativity.

2.3.2 Map overlay method

Overlay technique is sometimes also referred as McHarg's method. This methodology relies on a set of maps of environmental characteristics (physical, social, ecological, aesthetic) for a project area. These maps are overlaid to produce a composite characterization of the regional environment. Impacts are identified by noting the impacted environmental characteristics lying within the project boundaries.

This is a highly aggregative approach and is best suited to short list the alternatives where decision is mainly based on physical characteristics (Sondheim, 1978).

An example of effective use of McHarg's method is determination of areas to be avoided while locating during the course of a highway project in Maleysia (Nuruddin etal., 1987).

The approach seems most useful as a method for screening alternative sites or routes, preliminary to detailed impact analysis. Limitations of the approach include its inability to quantify as well as identify possible impacts and its failure in implicit weighting of all characteristics mapped. Use of the technique is possible only if suitable maps or data base adequate to draw maps exists in a country. This would be the primary difficulty in adopting this methodology in developing countries.

2.3.3 Matrices

While checklist are 'one dimensional' lists of potential impacts which tell whether an impact will occur or not, matrices are 'two dimensional' lists which also given an indication of the magnitude of the likely impacts. Matrices are thus checklists of a higher dimension and contain more information than the latter.

Broadly, matrices may be categorised in three different groups. Examples of the first category where magnitude of the relationship and importance are considered - are Leopold Matrix (Leopold et al, 1971), Fisher and Davies (Fisher, 1973) and Shopley and Fuggbe (Shopley, 1984). Extended Component Interaction Matrix comes under the second category. This matrix was developed to enable consideration of second and higher order impacts. In impact analysis, first order dependencies between the components are identified. The second and higher order impacts are then determined using matrix multiplication technique (Bisset, 1980).

A three dimensional matrix representing cause-effect matrix, cause-impact matrix, and effect-impact matrix was developed by Mongkol (1902); it comes under the third category of matrices. Here, the activities of the project are taken as causes, changes in resource relations and structures are taken as effects, and changes in quality of life, health, and productivity, etc., are considered as impacts.

Two dimensional matrices have been extensively used, and are continue to be so (AIL, 1990; NEERI, 1992 a-d; 1993; Sundaresan etal., 1989). In comparison matrices help in making qualitative judgment on the relationships among various parameters. They help to perceive and understand the complex interactions among the parameters. These are useful as preliminary assessment methods and are used as part of a comprehensive assessment. The matrix methods also find applications in cross-impact analysis, input-output analysis, and interpretive structural modelling. However, matrices cannot be used for identification of impacts. They operate only after the impacts are identified. And, when matrices are multiplied to get second and higher order impacts, the process becomes cumbersome.

A number of variations to the basic matrix approach described above have been used. Depending on how detailed the list of actions or effects is, what criteria are used to score impacts (magnitude, importance, duration, probability of occurrence, feasibility of mitigation), and what type of scale is used for scoring, quite different final impressions regarding severity of impact can be conveyed.

2.3.4 Delphi method

Delphi is a method based on intuition/expert opinion, especially designed to avoid the drawbacks associated with the other methods of opinion gathering.

Delphi has three special characteristics: (i) anonymity among participants, (ii) scope for statistical treatment of responses, and (iii) iterative feedback. A structured, formal and detailed questionnaire is given, by mail or in person. The different participants do not meet. The responses of the participants are analysed, combined, averaged, and represented in quartiles and medians. Question for the second round are then made, with modifications if necessary (as perceived by the programme director or the participants). the averaged responses to the first questionnaire are provided to the participants. Apart from the original questionnaire, the participants may be asked to respond to scaled objective items, and sometimes to open-ended responses. After scrutinizing the answers to the second round, respondents in the upper and lower quartiles may be asked to justify their responses. Further iterations are continued if necessary, to the point where diminishing returns set in. A convergence of opinion often emerges but the organisor of Delphi avoids forcing convergence or conditioning responses.

Delphi can be used to forecast technological or social events and policy shapes. It has following advantages over panels and surveys:

i) it can be used when the problem may not be amenable to analytical techniques, but solutions could be found from a subjective group judgment;
ii) it can be applied when issues are controversial and there are serious disagreements amongst experts;
iii) it can be applied when issues are of such a nature that individuals are unwilling to take a public stance; and
iv) it enables participation of greater number of individuals than can effectively interact in face-to-face meetings; or time and cost constraints make frequent meeting infeasible.

Although widely used (Abbasi 1995a; Abbasi & Vineethan, 1995). Delphi has been criticised on a number of grounds:

i) there is pressure towards convergence and this may suppress other valid perspectives;
ii) the role of the Delphi coordinator is crucial and subjective biases may be introduced through this route;
iii) lack of item clarity or common interpretation of scales and feedback may lead to invalid results; and
iv) it is time consuming and if the questionnaires are long, one may tend to fill them in a casual manner.

Delphi can be used in the early stages of EIA to identify the impacts and importance ratings of a new project for which readymade information are not available. The information obtained through Delphi method can, of course, be used as input to other methods

2.4 LESS COMMONLY USED METHODS

2.4.1 Content analysis

Content analysis is an extensive search of the related literature in order to enlist activities and their impacts. It can be useful if the project to be assessed and its setting are similar to the ones studied in the past. However such situations are rare.

2.4.2 Survey methods

Survey methods are used to collect opinion of a large number of respondents. These methods suffer from such shortcomings as researcher bias and respondent bias. But they are very useful when no recorded material is available about a system or about the perceptions of population in the system. There are several techniques listed under the category. Finsterbusch et at. (1983) list the following major survey methods:

i) face-to-face interview,
ii) telephone interview,
iii) self-administered questionnaire
iv) leave-and-pickup questionnaire, and
v) mail questionnaire.

This list is not exhaustive. Several new techniques, such as newspaper ballots and feedback mail, are evolving (Coats, 1976b).

Survey methods are useful to identify the issues and the impacts, and can involve a large number of people in the process. However, they are not useful during the other stages of EIA.

2.4.3 Strategic impact and assumptions identification method (SIAM)

SIAM was developed by Mason, Milroff and Eirshoff for socio-economic assessment (Abonyi, 1980, 1982). It helps to identify the impact, stakeholders in terms of inputs and outputs and the underlying assumption of the relationship between inputs/outputs and the stakeholders.

Then the assumptions are weighted based on which the issues and impacts are identified. These identified stakeholders are then involved in the EIA process.

SIAM is applied by Abonyi for Highway infrastructure assessment study (1980), and Lead-Zinc smelter project assessment study (1982). SIAM exercise deals mainly with the primary impacts. It is possible, and is often necessary, to deduce the secondary and tertiary impacts and the related assumptions.

2.4.4 Priority-trade off-scanning (PTS) approach

The priority-tradeoff-scanning approach was developed by Davos (1977) for the evaluation of options in environmental management. The method includes the development of the following three matrices:

i) the goal-achievement matrix (GAM),
ii) the goal-priority-tradeoff matrix (GPTM), and
iii) the interest-priority-tradeoff matrix (IPTM).

The goal-achievement matrix consists of the goals, their relative weights, costs, and benefits representing columns, and groups representing rows. These are determined for several groups of people. In the goal-priority-tradeoff matrix the priority of goals is determined and the alternative options are ranked for each goal by every group. The interest-priority-tradeoff matrix consists of groups both rowwise and columnwise. An element p_{ij} of the matrix is the option that the ith group is willing to accept when accounting for the interests of the jth group.

This method is essentially meant to deal with the various groups of people in collecting their perceptions or perspectives. It is particularly useful when the perspectives are highly divergent. Unlike in Delphi, no statistical analysis is used in this method; rather every group is presented with perceptions or ranking of the other groups and interest tradeoffs are developed to narrow down the divergence.

2.4.5 Sondheim method

A rating and weighting method was proposed by Sondheim in 1978, which includes a procedure to prepare rating and weighting matrices. These matrices are developed by two separate panels. Rating matrix ranks the alternatives and weighting matrix gives importance. A third matrix, decision matrix, is compiled by multiplying rating and weighting schemes.

It differs from matrix methods in the process of developing the matrix. However, it does not consider inter-relationships among the variables.

2.5 EMERGING METHODOLOGIES

2.5.1 Cross-impact analysis

This consists of a family of methods which study the effect of occurrence or non-occurrence of a set of events on the occurrence (or nonoccurrence) of the same events. In cross-impact analysis individual components are not only evaluated independently but also in relation to each others (Coats, 1976).

This is a means of utilising a matrix representation to analyse interactions between probable future events, or between elements of particular technological events. Elements or events to be analysed for interactions are arrayed in the first row and column of a matrix. Interaction between the elements is represented by means of a number which may reflect the importance of the interaction, probability of occurrence or other parameters of importance.

This procedure, if applied to all the events, takes a long time to estimate all conditional probabilities and is also very cumbersome to do. When fully and quantitatively implemented, cross-impact analysis requires considerable time and computer resources.

Examples of this category are ISM and MICMAC which are based on the analysis of inter-parameter relationship and classifies behaviour of variables.

2.5.2 Networks or impact tree analysis

Environmental sub-systems are interconnected and any impact on one of this subsystems effects several other subsystem. Thus a 'primary' impact leads to 'secondary', 'tertiary' and higher order impacts.

Network methods recognise this interactive nature of environmental components and take an ecological approach for identifying the secondary and tertiary impacts.

Network methods start with a list of project activities or actions and then generate cause-condition-effect networks(i.e., chains or events), thus taking into cognisance the fact that a series of impacts may be triggered by a project action. Hence, this method provides a road map type of approach to the identification of second-and third-order effects. The idea is to start with a project activity and identify the types of impacts which would initially occur. The next step is to select each impact and identify the impacts which may be induced as a result. This process is repeated until all possible impacts have been identified. Sketching this in network form results in what is commonly referred to as an *impact tree.* Figure 4 illustrates an 'impact tree' for a stream-bank stabilization project. One advantage of this type of approach is that it allows the user to identify impacts by selecting and tracing out the events as they might be expected to occur. A major problem in constructing cause-condition-effect networks is achieving the degree of detail necessary for informed decision making. On the other hand, if the environmental condition changes are described in detail and all possible inter-relationships are included, the resulting impact networks could be too extensive and complex to be really useful.

A method developed by Bardossy (1983) belongs to this category and has been applied to the Multi criteria decision making (MCDM) of water resources.

2.5.3 Modelling

A model may be defined as 'a mathematical, physical, electrical or any other form of representation which is intended to parallel or *mimic* in terms of structure, properties, or function some real world system'. As is most often used, a model consists of a set of structurally interrelated variables which are fitted into a set of mathematical equations and which are processed with the help of a computer. The variables chosen are those which quantify the various aspects of technological growth. The cause-effect relationships are expressed by means of the equation, and the input and system parameters change with the time dimension. To begin with a model is constructed on the basis of logical relationships and assumptions, and is tested against historical performance of the system. If disagreement occurs, sensitivity analyses are performed and model revised till actual past performance and model performance coincide. The model can then be run forward in time to obtain forecasts.

Modelling techniques give us an extremely powerful means of environmental impact analysis. The following drawbacks of modelling have been pointed out.

i) The construction of a formal model, complete with software and data base is very time-consuming and expensive.
ii) The nuances of a complex issue may not be adequately represented in a model.

iii) There may be a tendency to quantify factors which are intrinsically difficult to quantify.

iv) There is a danger that the model may be used as a substitute for critical thought and its output accepted without analysing the factors that led to it.

KSIM, GSIM and system dynamics are the examples of this category.

An evaluation of the methodologies on the basis of functional classification, nature of parameter estimation, subjectivity and computerization is presented in Table 2.1.

2.6 NEED OF COMPUTERIZATION

Thus, EIA is one of the major tools in environmental planning and management. The aim is to minimize the environmental degradation associated with unplanned human activities in the context of the existing political and socio-economic frameworks. However, When conducting environmental impact assessment of a multi-faceted project, one may come across a bewilderingly large number of possible quantifiable impacts. This makes identifying and assessing the environmental impacts an enormously complex task. To quote:

> "...as a science, EIA is as multidisciplinary, interdisciplinary and transdisciplinary as environment itself because all aspects and `dimensions' of environment - physical, biological, social, temporal, economic,... to name a few, have to be studied and weighted in EIA..." (Pg. 1)
>
> *(Abbasi, 1993a)*

Identification and assessment procedures of various impacts therefore require collection and manipulation of large amounts of data, and more importantly, communicating the final results to decision-makers and members of the public in a manner intelligible to them as many of them are unlikely to be experts in environmental sciences. To overcome these difficulties, considerable attention has been devoted to develop computer-aided structured approaches to

Table 2.1: Summarty of EIA Methodologies

	Functional Classifications							Nature of parameter extimation			Sub-jecti-vity			Comput-eriza-tion	
	Evaluation of alternatives	Impact identification	Causality identification	Prediction / Estimation	Structuring the problem	Evaluation of interrelations	Behavioural categorization	Qualitative	Quantitaive	Both	Subjective	Objective	Rapidness of application	Easy	Complex
Commonly used methodlogies															
1. Checklist		X						X			X				
2. Overlays	X			X								X			
3. Matrices	X		X	X				X			X		X	X	
4. Expert opinion		X	X					X			X		X		
Less commonly used methodologies															
5. Content analysis		X	X								X				
6. Survey methods		X	X					X			X				
7. Delphi		X	X	X				X			X				X
8. SIAM		X									X				
9. Priority-tradeoff -scanning method	X							X			X		X		X
10. Sondheim method	X							X							
Emerging methodologies															
11. Cross impact analysis			X			X		X				X	X	X	
12. ISM					X							X	X	X	
13. MICMAC method	X	X	X		X		X	X				X	X	X	
14. Networks	X	X	X	X					X			X	X		X
15. KSIM	X		X	X	X	X				X		X			X
16. System dynamics	X		X	X	X	X				X		X			X

assessment;, commonly called EIA methodologies or methods. Computer based approaches can effectively handle the immense data of an EIA study, and can do the analysing and assessing in a much shorter time than otherwise.

A Computer based approach can also provide a powerful interactive tool for managers and planners, regulators and policy makers, because it makes access to a large number of relevant database, problem simulation methods and decision support tools. The thesis proposes some frameworks for computer-aided EIA and demonstrate their applicability as effective and swift tools

2.7 ANALYSIS FRAMEWORK

The existing methodologies have some advantages; they also suffer from major shortcomings. Attempts to overcome these shortcomings has led to search of newer techniques and development of newer methods. The review reveals that:

i) thus far most of the '*emerging*' methodologies have not been able to stand the test of extensive field trials; in other words these methodologies are largely confined to paper;
ii) the reasons for this, essentially, are that most of the newer methodologies either require information on the precise nature of inter-parameter relationships (which simply are not available in most cases), or they are computationally or experimentally too cumbersome (and/or unwieldy or costly) to be of much practical utility;
iii) no single *system* of methodologies is available which enables all the three stages of EIA to be accomplished viz a) identification of parameters to be studied b) assessment of their trends and c) impact summation; and
iv) '*as a whole*' assessment of an environmental system and analysis of developmental policies are not carried out in such a way that planners and policy makers - who are unlikely to be the subject experts - could understand the results.

We have made attempts to develop methodologies to overcome some of the abovementioned shortcomings. A system of three methodologies has been developed which may enable all the three stages of EIA to be accomplished. It includes :

i) a formulation and software package INTRA for the identification of key parameters out of a large number one invariably encounters during any EIA. It also helps us in arranging the influencing parameters in the order of their importance to generate a hierarchical structure. We hope that such a methodology would help us in understanding the nature, directions and importance of the influence of various parameters enabling us to determine which ones play a dominant role and which ones are merely peripheral;

ii) a designer software package incorporating the tests and tools needed to process basic data pertaining to typical EIA; and

iii) a methodology and software package to integrate the individual environmental impacts for generating net impact scores. This system also enables generation of scenarios and deciding which of the scenarios are environmentally viable.

Three computer software packages INTRA (INTer-parameter Relationship Analysis), SMART-ALEC (Statistical Measurement for Assessing Regional Trends - And Longterm Environmental Consequences) and CREAM (Computer-aided Rapid impact Evaluation And Management) have also been developed for each step of the proposed EIA system.

3

BACKDROP FOR TESTING THE NEW METHODOLOGIES

3.1 INTRODUCTION

In this chapter we are presenting the study area used for demonstrating the methodologies developed by us. The study area is the small city of Roorkee situated in the State of Uttar Pradesh, India (Figure 3.1).

Roorkee is a flower-shaped town spread over a flat terrain with the grand spectacle of Himalayan ranges flanking it in the East and the North-east. The dominant feature of the town is the Upper Ganges Canal which flows north-south and bisects the town. The canal has elevated embankments flanked with huge masonry lions.

Roorkee lies at 29 51'N Latitude and 77 53'E Longitude in Uttar Pradesh, 274 meters above mean sea level. The town has an administrative status of a Tehsil (sub-division). It lies 172 kilometers North of Delhi on the Delhi-Dehradun-Mussoorie Highway. Another Highway, 55 km Roorkee-Hardwar-Rishikesh road links Roorkee to the Pilgrimage centres of Badrinath, Kedarnath, Gangotri and Yamunotri. Roorkee's location at the junction of highways leading to Hardwar, Badrinath, Dehradun and Mussoorie, attracts to it copious tourist traffic.

We have chosen Roorkee as a test-case primarily for the following reasons:

i) its cultural and political ethos, its multi-religion mix, and its distinct layers of socio-economic strata are all representative of typical Indian cities; indeed of all typical Asian cities;
ii) it is not a heavily industrialised city; therefore the impacts of industrialisation do not dominate the city's system but are among the several other contributory factors. In this respect too, the city is representative of a very large number of similar urban systems;
iii) all three predominant season - summer, winter, and monsoon - are witnessed in Roorkee;
iv) eventhough it is a major educational and tourist attraction, the city does not have significant floating population; and
v) basic data of adequate depth and reliability is available for this city albeit in diverse and difficult-to-access sources.

3.2 HISTORY

Roorkee is named after Ruri, the wife of a Rajput chieftain. It was believed to be the capital of a pargana in the time of Mughal Emperor Akbar, and finds a mention as such in *Ain-a-Akbari,* but there seems to be no evidence of old buildings of that time. When, in 1842 the transformation of Roorkee to its present status began, it was but a tiny hamlet comprising of mud huts.

From about the middle of the 18th century Roorkee was included in the estate of the Gujars of Landhaura, a place about 6 kilometers in the East and remained in their possession till Raja Ramdayal died in 1813. The town and seventeen dependent villages were then settled with the old Rajput proprietors, though no inquiry was made into individual rights either on that occasion or at subsequent settlements. In 1838, thirteen villages were settled with the Roorkee zamindars and in two other settlements the villages were awarded a *malikana* of five percent on the revenue.

In the beginning of 19th century, Roorkee was chosen for the location of a cantonment by the then, British, rulers. The event that heralded the transformation of Roorkee - construction of

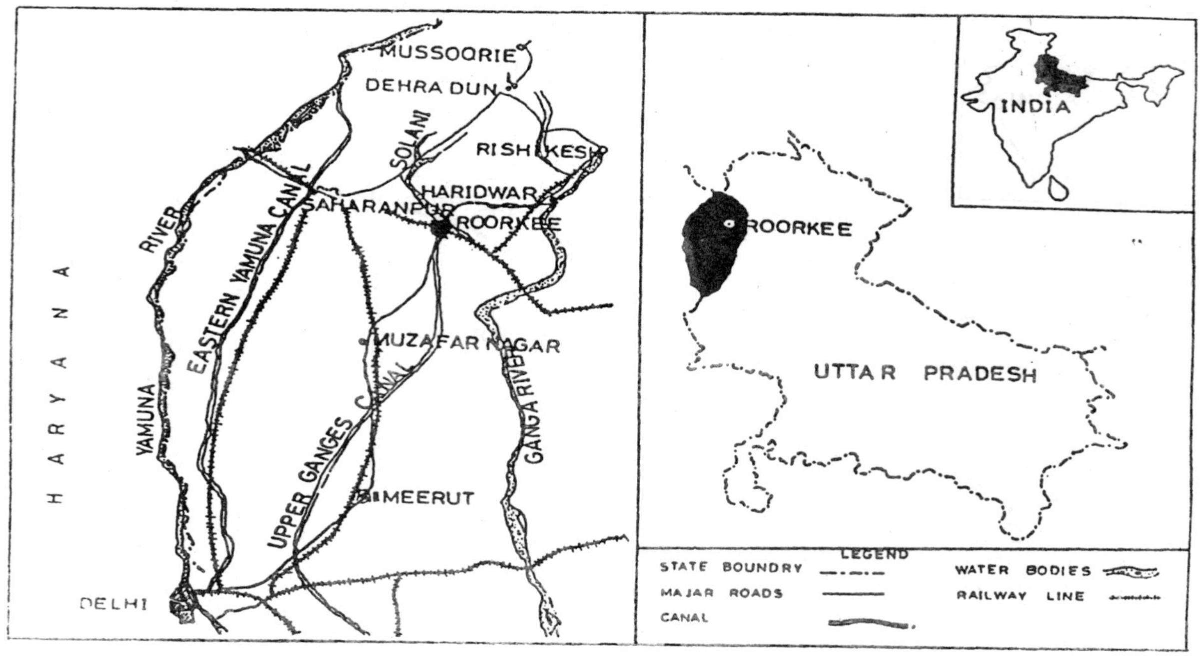

Figure 3.1: Location of Roorkee

Ganges Canal - began in 1842. What compelled the British to take up this project was the lessons they learnt from the 1833 famine in Guntoor. The famine caused the colonial rulers a loss of revenue to the tune of 66 lakh rupees-a colossal sum in those days. To pre-empt recurrence of such disaster in the Northern India, Thomason, the then Lieutenant Governor, mooted the idea of the ganges canal. He wrote to the Governor-General to on 3 September 1846: as follows:

"If the undertaking (the Ganges Canal) had been merely of display, or even of doubtful utility, it could not be recommended in the present state of the finances; but it is in fact an economical measure, necessary for the stability of the revenue, and is therefore the more deserving of consideration in proportion to the very pressure upon the finances, if only the money can be obtained. Providentially, there has not lately been any great calamity in the districts which will be affected by the canal similar to that of 1837, which cost the government a million sterling, as well as the lives of thousands of its subjects; but such events may any day occur. Even in the ordinary course, the state annually looses all the advantage which must arise from increased cultivation, greater wealth and a denser population."

To look after the maintenance of canal the Canal Workshop and Iron Foundry were established in 1852 in the civil lines on the canal bank. This was followed by the establishment of Civil Engineering School, later known as Thomason College of Civil Engineering. In 1853, Bengal Sappers and Minors were stationed here, which provided a controlling influence during the 1857 uprising (Nevill 1921). Some other important events in the history of Roorkee are recounted below.

1. Under the post office act 1866, it was among the first few towns to have a post office and first telegraphic office in the district.
2. In the year 1886, Roorkee was placed on the Railway map of India.
3. In 1907, first provincial trunk road - Meerut-Roorkee-Dehradun - was constructed.
4. In 1920, Roorkee became the first town in Uttar Pradesh to have Hydel electricity.

5. In 1949, Thomason College of Civil Engineering was elevated as University of Roorkee, becoming the first engineering university of India.

3.3 URBANISATION AND ROORKEE

Roorkee was a very modest mud-built hamlet in the 19 century with a population of 5,511 in 1847 (Nevill 1921). It was resurrected from this non-descript position by the construction of the Upper Ganges Canal (during 1842-1854) and the concomitant establishment of Thomason College of Civil Engineering (in 1847). A steady growth of the town occurred around these two establishments till 1950. Then Thomason College was raised to the status of a university. This event stimulated the urbanisation of Roorkee as several new institutions came to be established in the proximity of the university, notably Central Building Research Institute, Irrigation Research Institute and National Institute of Hydrology. This growth in higher education, unusually rapid for a town by Indian standards, gave boost to the general growth and development of other sectors as well as the town.

By and by Roorkee became known in academic circles the world over as University of Roorkee is not only the first engineering university of India but one of the few of its type in Asia. As the university was a catalyst in the establishment of other R & D institutions of national importance, Roorkee rapidly became one of foremost educational and research centres in India.

The development of Roorkee in this manner had another interesting fall-out. A national highway was constructed to link Roorkee with Delhi which was extended to Mussoorie and Rishikesh (Figure 3.1). This made Roorkee a major tourist centre as the town became a key transition point for tourists going to Hardwar, Dehradun, Mussoorie, Badrinath, Kedarnath, Gangotri, Yamunotri, and Piran Kaliyar.

These events led to a transformation of Roorkee from an earlier concentric zone compact grained settlement to a multiple nuclei based compact grained settlement. A five-fold increase occurred in the population, associated with changes in sex ratio, literacy ratio, medical facilities, infrastructural facilities, occupational status, financial receipts and expenditure. The quantum of waste produced and manner of its disposal also changed appreciably.

3.4 CLIMATE

The climate of Roorkee is typical of Northwestern India, with very hot summers and very cold winters. Being a submontanic district, with a higher latitude than any other portion of the plains, it has longer spells of cold weather then Delhi. Though the heat in May and June is considerable, relief is occasionally afforded by the cooling effect of moderate Himalayan storms, the influence of which extends for some distance to the South. In terms of average annual precipitation (110 cm), Roorkee is semi-arid. The South-West monsoon generally breaks in mid-June and the North-East during November-December.

Winters begin from late September and continue through February. The coldest months are generally December and January, when the minimum temperature approaches zero.

A rise in temperature is experienced from the beginning of March, which heralds the onset of summer. During summer, the humidity

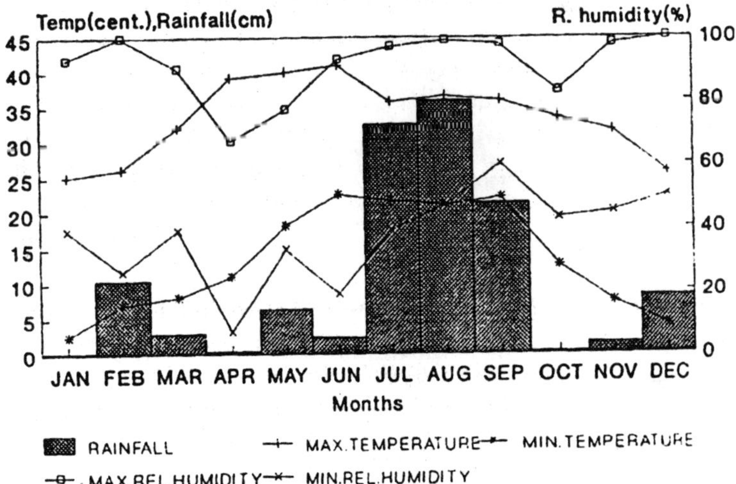

Figure 3.2: Pattern of climate in Roorkee in 1990

is around 10% during days. The day temperature is around 40 c and warm winds blow frequently.

Annual variation in climate typified by 1990 observations is presented in Figure 3.2.

3.5 THE TRENDS IN URBANISATION

3.5.1 Physical Growth

i) Area

The town (Roorkee) encompasses an area of 16.84 km (MB 1990). This includes 8.7 km of the cantonment area.

ii) Administrative affairs

As per the provisions of the Towns Act XX of 1856, Roorkee was given the status of a town in May 1860. Based on the provision of income categories as per Municipalities Act XXVI of 1850, it attained different classifications through the years (Table 3.1).

Table 3.1 :
Categorisation of Roorkee over the years on the bases of its municipal income

Year	Income range (Rs)	Class of Municipality
1879	Less than 50000	Class-IV
1937	50000 - 100000	Class-III
1947	100000 - 500000	Class-II
1957	More than 500000	Class-I

(SOURCES : Municipal board and cantonment board, Roorkee)

Upto 1879 the affairs of the cantonment and the rest of the town were overseen by a joint board. Thereafter two separate bodies, Municipal Board and Cantonment Board were created to look after the two major segments of Roorkee.

iii) Municipal limits

Till 1921, the municipal limits of Roorkee extended upto river Solani in the North, railway line in the South and Government Workshop, Thomason College of Civil Engineering and Cantonment on the East (Nevill 1921). In 1950 Ramnagar Colony was passed on to the Municipal Board by Rehabilitation Department, and the campus of Central Building Research Institute came up in 1965.

The next phase of the extension is proposed to bring six villages - Ibrahimpur, Matlabpur, Rampur and Sunahra in the Western side, Salempur in the South-west side and Khanjarpur in the East side - within the bounds of Roorkee. The extension is expected to come through in the near future.

iv) Settlement pattern

Till the early 19th century, Roorkee was merely a conglomeration of mud houses scattered over a large area in the form of hamlets with its core being *mohalla* (neighborhood) Rajputana but in the mid 20th century Civil Lines became the focal point of the expanding settlement. The patterns of this settlement from the days of the British rule to the present have been traced chronologically in Figure 3.3.

v) Administrative subdivision of Roorkee

Before independence there were no formal administrative sub-divisions existing in Roorkee. Only the broad categorisation in terms of 'old Roorkee' and 'new Roorkee' or 'Civil Lines' was in vogue.

After independence Roorkee was organized into 21 *mohallas.* Census records are available for these *mohallas* from 1951 onwards. In 1961 Ramnagar colony which had come up from the settlement of immigrants became the 22nd *mohalla.* The city was also organized into wards, the number of which increased with time. At present the city has 19 wards. The predominant communities (50% or more) of each ward and their economic status are conveyed in Table 3.2.

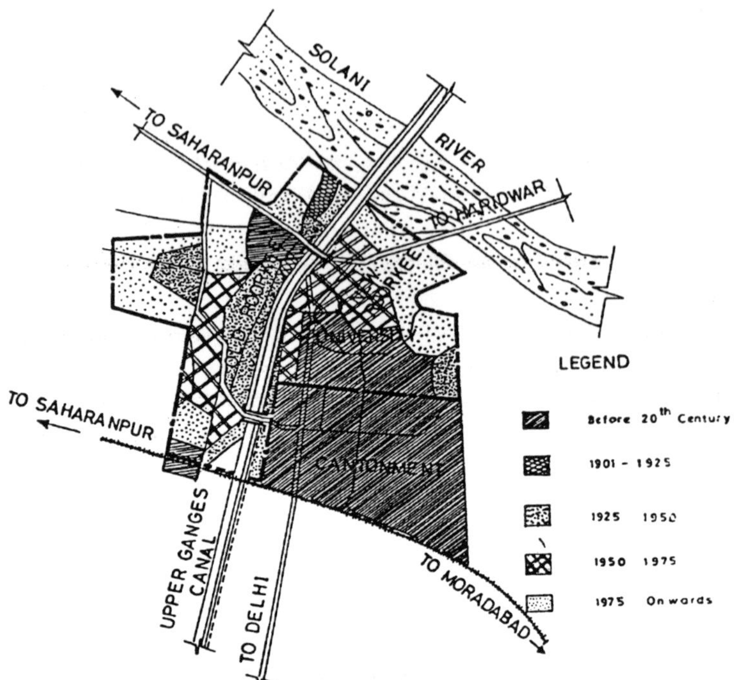

Fig. 3.3: Settlement pattern during the 19th and 20th centuries

vi) Demographic pattern before 20th century

The population of Roorkee slowly but substantially increased during 19th century except in the census year 1865 (Table 3.3). Some fluctuations during 1853-1872 occurred due to the highly instable condition of the region at that period especially after the 1857 War of Independence. A steady growth during 1872-1891 may be attributed to natural increase as also migration from nearby places. All in all, there was an increase of 215.13% during the period 1847-1891.

vii) Demographic pattern during the present century

The population figures are presented in Table 3.4. There was a decrease during 1901-1911 and a steep increase during 1931-1941. The former was the result of famine and epidemic which occurred during 1899, whereas an extraordinary increase in the male population of the cantonment area due to the onset of the second world war resulted in the latter. The rapid increase during 1951 to 1971 occurred with the growth in educational sector following the establishment of University of Roorkee and the development of other R&D institutions around it. Overall the population has increased by a whopping 484.52% so far in the 20th century.

TABLE 3.2 :
The ward-wise distribution of predominant economic and religious communities in Roorkee

Ward no.	Predominant mohalla	Predominant community*	Predominant income group
1	Purva vali	Mix	Middle
	Sheikh Puri	Mix	high
3	Chowmandi	Hindu	Mix
4	Ambartalab East	Mix	High & upper
5	Ambartalab East	Mix	Middle
6	Maqtoolpuri	Mix	Middle
7	Ramnagar	Migrants Class	Middle(Business)
8	Ramnagar	Migrants Class	Middle(Business)
9	Ambertalab west	Muslims	Middle & Low
10	Ambertalab west	Muslims	Middle & Low
11	Purani Tehsil	Mix	Middle & Low
12	Mahigran	Muslims	Middle & Low
13	Satti & Sot	Muslims	Middle & Low
14	Subzimandi	Muslims	Middle
15	Rajputana	Mix	Upper Middle
16	Civil Line	Mix	High
17	University	Mix	Mix
18	University	Mix	Mix
19	C.B.R.I Colony	Mix	Mix

* The community has been indicated where it exceeds 50%.
(SOURCE : Based on survey)

3.5.2 Health, education and recreational facilities

i) Health

The first official medical facility in Roorkee was established in 1850 in the form of Ganges Canal Dispensary. By and by Military Hospital, University Hospital and CBRI's Employee's State Insurance Dispensary were established (Figure 3.4).

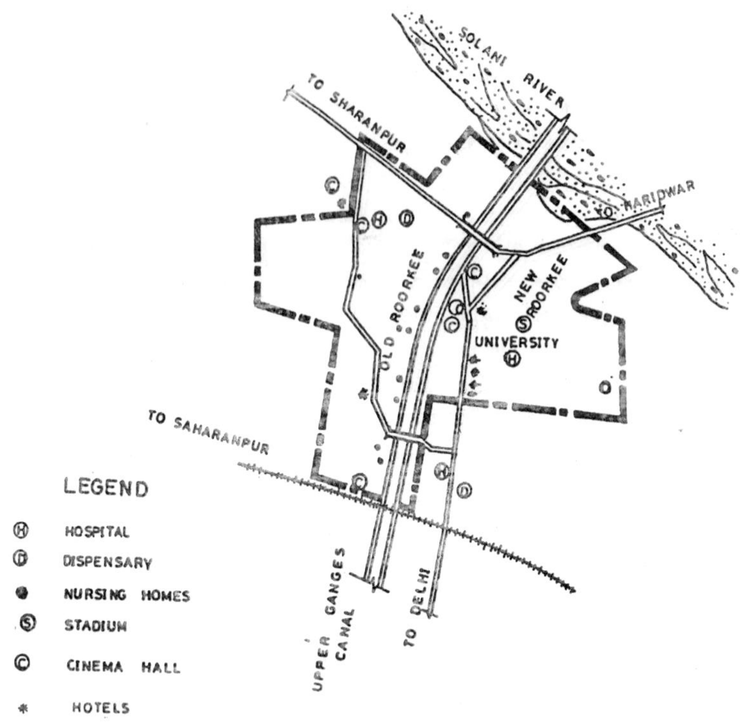

Fig. 3.4: Health and recreational facilitites in Roorkee

During the last decade (1980-1990) there has been substantial qualitative as well as quantitative improvement in health care. Larger number of doctors, encompassing broader spectrum of medical disciplines are now available. The Civil Hospital has been shifted to a new building and renamed *Jagdish Narayan Sinha Civil Hospital.* The number of medical practitioners of all levels, nursing homes, and maternity centers have also increased considerably (Table 3.5).

In its efforts towards maintaining a healthy environment, Municipal Board has been regularly conducting sanitation programs. The Municipal Board has also been organizing camps for administering vaccines for various diseases. During 1988, '89 and '90, the vaccines administered against Cholera were 777, 1956 and 69 respectively and against BCG 442, 283 and 337 respectively. No death was recorded due to these diseases (MB 1990).

Table 3.3 :
Demographic pattern of Roorkee in the 19th Century

Year	Population	Variation with respect to previous census	
		Absolute figure	%
1847	5511	-	-
1853	8592	+3081	+55.90
1865	7588	-1004	-11.69
1872	10778	+3190	+42.04
1881	15953	+5181	+48.07
1891	17367	+1414	+08.86

TABLE 3.4:
Demographic pattern of Roorkee in the 20th Century

Year	Population	Variation with respect to previous census	
		Absolute figure	%
1901	17148	-	-
1911	16584	-564	-03.29
1921	16716	+132	+00.80
1931	17476	+760	+04.55
1941	27364	+9888	+56.58
1951	33092	+5728	+20.93
1961	45801	+12709	+38.41
1971	62456	+16655	+36.36
1981	79076	+16620	+26.61
1991	100236	+21160	+26.75

The present status of water works of Roorkee is summarized in Table 3.8 (UP Jal Nigam, 1989).

ii) Education

Before the foundation of Thomason College of Civil Engineering in 1847, there were only *maktabs* or *pathshalas* (primary schools) in Roorkee to impart education. In 1851, with the establishment of *Tehsil School*, vernacular education was started. This was followed by an Anglo-Vernacular school in 1856. Municipal and mission schools were added in 1872. The first girls' school was started by the Arya Samaj in 1907 (Nevill 1921).

TABLE 3.5 :
Existing medical facilities in Roorkee

1.	Doctors(MBBS)	61
2.	Doctors(BAMS)	12
3.	Dentists	5
4.	Surgeons	5
5.	Bone specialists	4
6.	Eye specialists	3
7.	ENT surgeon	1
8.	Gynaecologists	7
9.	Anesthesiologist	1
10.	Cardiologists	3
11.	Child specialist	6
12.	General Physicians	17
13.	Pathologists	4
14.	Radiologists	5
15.	Hospitals	3
16.	Dispensary	2
17.	Nursing homes	14
18.	Beds(Total)	500
19.	Medical stores	35

(SOURCE : Based on survey)

A steady progress has been maintained in providing more avenues of education. As already discussed, the establishment of University of Roorkee as a major engineering university after independence has given a great impetus to post-school education in Roorkee. The educational institutions functioning at present in Roorkee are enumerated in Table 3.6.

iii) Recreational facilities

Considering the extent of growth in population, tourist traffic, and the presence in its midst of renowned educational institutions, Roorkee presents a dismal picture with respect to availability of recreational facilities.

TABLE 3.6 :
Institutions of higher education in Roorkee

Level	Numbers
University	1
Degree College(Arts/Science)	3
Pohytechnic	1
Higher Secondary/Intermediate schools	5
Secondary/Matriculation schools	8
Junior Secondary & Middle Schools	12

(SOURCE : Based on survey)

TABLE 3.7 :
Recreational facilities existing in Roorkee

Particulars	Numbers
Cinema halls	6
Clubs	3
Boat club	1
Swimming pools	2
Stadiums	3
Children's parks	6
Hotels	7

(SOURCE : Based on survey)

Eventhough Roorkee University and Cantonment - both having a stadium of their own - are well-endowed in terms of sport facilities and cultural activities, these are available only to persons belonging to these institutions and are out of bounds for other residents of Roorkee. For the latter Ganges Canal and Nehru Stadium are the only two avenues for outdoor recreation. The town gets its indoor entertainment from television and video. Prior to the advent of VCPs, cinema halls were very popular but now there is such a decline in the patronage of theater-goers that some halls have closed down (Table 3.7).

3.5.3 Urban services

i) Water supply

The first municipal water-works covering the then entire town of Roorkee were commissioned in 1954-55. These supplies were based on bore-wells. Prior to that open dug wells had been the main source of domestic water in Roorkee. These wells were either owned by individuals or were provided for community use by the government.

Eventhough large quantities of water flow through Roorkee every moment in the Ganges Canal, these waters are not available to the residents of Roorkee, being earmarked to serve the irrigation needs of people living several kilometer downstream. An attempt was made in 1930 by the Thomason College to run a small water supply unit based on the Canal but the attempt was soon abandoned.

ii) Water quality testing

Presently, testing of water quality is irregular and only very few samples are collected, randomly, from the city by the Public Health Authority. These are transported to the State Health Organization, Lucknow, for analysis. The results of the tests conducted during 1987-89 are given in Table 3.9 (MB 1990). The only treatment done for purifying the water is chlorination.

iii) Drainage and sanitation

The topography of Roorkee is such that it facilitates natural drainage. The *nallahs* efficiently drain-off rainwater and sullage to the river Solani. The streets are provided with open drains leading to the low lands. These drains are regularly cleaned and flushed.

The collection and disposal of wastes is done by a mixed system of conservatory and sewer lines, but the former is predominant. About 70 % of the town area is sewered; the number of connections being–1900 (Figure 3.5).

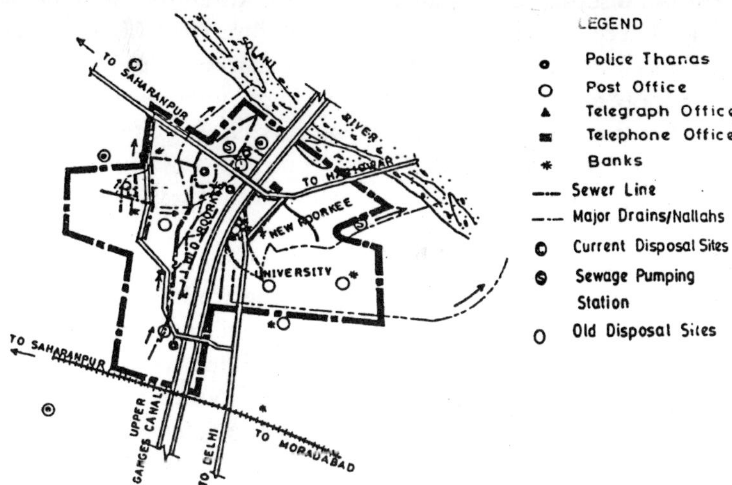

Fig. 3.5: Location of essential services in Roorkee

Two 25 BHP sewage pumping stations, one on the Rampur road in *mohalla Mahigran* and other in village Khanjarpur, divert raw sewage of the town for direct agricultural applications without treatment.

During the last decade Health Department constructed 5 public latrines and 17 public toilets at different places in the city.

The university has its own system of waste collection. It has two tractors for collecting garbage, which is disposed at the disposal site of Municipal Board. Raw sewage from university after collection is diverted to the sewage pumping station at Khanjarpur which pumps it to the disposal site of Saliyar Village.

CBRI was using its garbage for the purpose of land filling in its residential colony till 1987. Now the institute has entered into a contract with Roorkee Municipality for collection of garbage. The sewage generated at CBRI, after collection in a sump well, is diverted to Khanjarpur pumping station.

For the disposal of garbage/solid wastes, three sites were being used till recently :(i) near *Idgah* on Sunehra road (ii) in village Padli and (iii) near *subzimandi* (vegetable market). Due to increase in the waste quantity as a result of growing population and human settlements coming up around these sites, a new site at Saliyar village was established in 1982. The site encompasses approximately 5 acres. Earlier, waste used to lie openly until it was collected by tractors. With better facilities now, sub-collection sites have been established and the collection has been streamlined through the use of Double Wheel Beroge and Telecone trolleys. In addition, solid waste/garbage is also collected from the main market daily morning using tractor and trolleys. About 6 Telecone trolleys and 7 tractor trolleys (including 2 of University of Roorkee) full of waste reach the dumping site everyday. By a conservative estimate 150-200 tones of solid waste is dumped each day. Auctioning of the compost from this disposal site is done annually during March-May, generating revenue of the order of Rs 50,000.

TABLE 3.8 :
Existing water works in Roorkee

Category of water works	:	'C'
No.of Tube wells	:	10
Total water available from tube wells/day	:	22772.6 kl
Supply in terms of lpcd	:	367.8
Supply in terms of hrs/day	:	19
No.of elevated tanks	:	5
Capacity	:	450 kl
		1700 kl
		750 kl
		495 kl
		2500 kl
No. of connections	:	6697
Length of Water supply line	:	63.00km

(SOURCE : MB 1990)

iv) Electrification

Roorkee and Hardwar were the first two towns of Uttar Pradesh to get Hydel Electricity, after construction of Bahadarabad power house in 1926. Prior to that there was no electrical supply and oil lamps were used for lighting (Nevill 1921).

Table 3.9:
Water quality sampling done by the Roorkee municipality

Year	No.of samples	Reports
1987-88	4	Satisfactory
1988-89	2	1 sample satisfactory
1989-90	4	3 samples satisfactory

v) Cooking gas

Cooking gas has been used in Roorkee since 1970-71 with the establishment of Roorkee gas agency. In 1984 Deepali gas service came into existence and Chavi gas agency started functioning in 1990. These agencies have distributed over 18000 connections in the town so far.

vi) Road links

The first metalled road in Roorkee, linking the railway station and the town, was constructed in 1914 (Nevill 1921). During 1918-21, several streets and bye-lanes were lined with *kankar* (gravel) and brick. Open drains were provided along the sides of these roads to effect drainage. Cement concreting of the streets began after independence and was completed by 1954.

At present Roorkee has 41.011 km of metalled roads, 97.001 km of semi-metalled roads and 5.731 kilometer of earthen roads (MB 1990).

3.5.4 Institutional growth

The premier institutions which have played very significant role in the development of Roorkee, and the years of their establishment, are :

Government Workshops	:	1843
Thomason College of Civil Engineering	:	1847
Cantonment (Bengal Engineers Group Headquarter)	:	1853
University of Roorkee	:	1949

Central Building Research Institute	:	1951
Irrigation Research Institute	:	1953
Structural Engineering Research Centre	:	1965
National Institute of Hydrology	:	1979
World Bank Canal Project	:	1984

i) Government (Ganges Canal) Workshop

We have dwelt upon the history of Ganges Canal and its role in catalysing the growth of Roorkee. The establishment of Government Workshop in 1843 was a direct offshoot of the Canal. The workshop, in turn, provided the impetus for the establishment of Thomason College of Engineering (in 1847). The chain of events continued with the formation of University of Roorkee and establishment around the university of several premier engineering institutions. The institutional growth in turn led to the growth of Roorkee town.

The workshop is located on the left bank of the Ganges Canal in between the city bridge and Solani river aqueduct. Originally as the canal foundry and workshop, it had a moderate beginning in 1843 to house a timber yard, a smithy shop and a carpentry shop for the canal. By 1848 it had developed as a full-fledged workshop with lathes and other machinery.

In 1852 the workshop became an independent and self supporting establishment. In 1903 it passed on to private ownership but was re-acquired by the Government in 1943. The workshop conducts repairs and manufacturing jobs for various Government Departments and is under the administrative control of Industries Department, Uttar Pradesh.

ii) Cantonment (Bengal Engineers Group and Head quarter)

Bengal Engineers Group was initially set up at Kanpur in 1803. It was reorganized in 1819 as the Corps of Bengal Sappers and Minors. In 1853 it was shifted to Roorkee.

TABLE 3.10 :
Minimum and maximum temperature (°C)

Year	Maximum	Minimum	Year	Maximum	Minimum
1950	41.7	2.2	1973	45.0	1.0
1951	44.4	3.8	1974	45.0	1.0
1952	44.4	4.4	1975	44.0	3.0
1953	44.4	2.8	1976	43.0	3.0
1954	44.4	1.7	1977	45.0	2.0
1955	41.0	0.6	1978	47.0	2.0
1956	45.6	2.8	1979	46.0	3.0
1957	44.7	3.6	1980	43.0	4.0
1958	45.6	3.6	1981	41.1	1.3
1959	44.6	4.1	1982	42.0	2.2
1960	45.6	3.0	1983	43.0	3.0
1961	44.4	3.6	1984	45.0	3.0
1962	44.6	1.9	1985	43.0	1.0
1963	42.2	2.7	1986	43.0	2.0
1964	43.1	-0.2	1987	46.0	4.0
1965	46.1	1.3	1988	46.0	1.0
1966	46.0	1.1	1989	48.0	1.0
1967	45.0	1.0	1990	46.7	2.2
1968	44.0	1.9	1991	45.6	1.8
1969	45.1	1.1	1992	46.0	2.0
1970	43.1	1.2	1993	45.0	2.3
1971	41.1	1.3	1994	44.0	1.6
1972	43.0	1.1			

(SOURCES : IMD 1988,1991,1992,1993,1994)

The cantonment roads have been laid in grid pattern with two main roads running through North to South, one of which is the Delhi-Dehradun Grant-trunk road. The central road running East to West leads to Railway station.

As the cantonment does not have any major shopping centre, it has to depend on the town for its supplies. This has indirectly boosted the local economy.

iii) Thomason College of Civil Engineering and University of Roorkee

When it was established in 1847, Thomason College of Civil Engineering had three departments with an intake of 30 students. Subsequently, in 1875, the intake was increased to 126. By the close of the nineteenth century many new courses such as mechanical and electrical apprenticeship were added. New technical workshop and laboratories were constructed. The total number of students in 1906 was 496 of whom 414 were Indians. In 1914 a textile course was opened which was transferred to Kanpur in 1920. From 1920 mechanical and electrical courses were stopped. During the Second World War (1943) School of Military Engineering was established which was later shifted to Poona in 1947 (UOR 1967). During 1947-52 the college housed the uprooted Punjab Engineering College and sustained it, till it was shifted back to its own premises at Chandigarh. Thus Thomason College of Engineering has served as a nursery for several major engineering institutions in India.

In 1949 the College was raised to the status of a University with Dr. C.A.Hart as its first Vice-Chancellor. From then on the institution has kept soaring to increasingly greater heights of achievement. Major expansion of the postgraduate engineering courses, establishment of the departments of Sciences and Architecture, and foresighted diversification of research and training programs in inter-disciplinary fields - notably Water Resources Development and Earthquake Engineering - has given Roorkee university the stature of a premier educational institution of the world.

At present Roorkee university offers 10 undergraduate courses in engineering and architecture and over 50 postgraduate courses in engineering, architecture, sciences, and technology. Ph.D. programs are available in a large number of disciplines, appropriately buttressed by requisite advanced courses wherever necessary.

The campus is spread over a scenic area of 150 hectares and has additional 10 hectare at its Institute of Paper Technology Campus. Visitors to the campus are often enchanted by the architectural elegance of the main building, spacious lawns and itsgardens. The University being fully residential, its campus hums with sports and cultural activities.

As regards the impact of Roorkee University on the growth of Roorkee, it may be mentioned that nearly all the developmental and commercial activity in the Civil Lines was a direct consequence of the growth of the University and its sister institutions.

iv) Central Building Research Institute (CBRI)

CBRI is a research laboratory of the Council of Scientific and Industrial Research (CSIR). This lab was established as a research unit in 1949 but was raised to the status of an institute of national importance in 1951.

CBRI is situated south-east of Roorkee University. Presently it forms part of the Roorkee Municipal Board but till 1965 it was reckoned as part of village Khanjarpur.

The institute acts as a R&D lab as well as advisory and consulting body to governmental organizations, industries, and all those connected with the building industry.

CBRI has its own residential colony, junior-level high school, hostels, dispensary, and other essential infrastructural facilities.

v) Structural Engineering Research Centre (SERC)

SERC was a section of CBRI till 1965 after which it evolved into an independent organization. Recently it has been shifted to Ghaziabad (UP).

vi) Irrigation Research Institute

Irrigation Research Institute (IRI) is situated on the right bank of the Ganges Canal. The institute was first started in 1947 at Bahadarabad (17 km from Roorkee on Roorkee-Hardwar Road). It was shifted to Roorkee partly in 1949 and completely by 1953.

The institute has two main offices. One is engaged in research and the other in design. The Institute is fully equipped with advanced machinery and apparatus to deal with research related to hydraulics and hydraulic structures.

TABLE 3.11:
Annual total rainfall (mm)

Year	Rainfall	Year	Rainfall	Year	Rainfall
1902	1099	1934	917	1966	1282
1903	961	1935	512	1967	1310
1904	946	1936	1362	1968	688
1905	797	1937	1011	1969	958
1906	1473	1938	871	1970	732
1907	646	1939	785	1971	1703
1908	978	1940	1119	1972	1011
1909	1043	1941	658	1973	1451
1910	1420	1942	2306	1974	1400
1911	1134	1943	1007	1975	1360
1912	1103	1944	913	1976	1497
1913	717	1945	1530	1977	1644
1914	1392	1946	1050	1978	1790
1915	1037	1947	1248	1979	754
1916	1225	1948	1333	1980	990
1917	960	1949	1329	1981	907
1918	521	1950	1376	1982	899
1919	1257	1951	821	1983	1168
1920	1010	1952	900	1984	789
1921	977	1953	995	1985	833
1922	1191	1954	1097	1986	741
1923	1256	1955	1348	1987	1070
1924	1562	1956	1832	1988	1400
1925	903	1957	1361	1989	1002
1926	1013	1958	1370	1990	1236
1927	852	1959	1427	1991	1300
1928	919	1960	957	1992	1080
1929	633	1961	1256	1993	1100
1930	939	1962	1029	1994	1280
1931	899	1963	1220		
1932	1258	1964	1368		

(SOURCES : IMD 1988, 1991, 1992, 1993, 1994)

The institute has its own residential colony situated on either side of the Ganges Canal.

vii) National Institute of Hydrology (NIH)

NIH, established in 1979, is a premier institution for R&D and extension relating to hydrology. It is sponsored by Ministry of Water Resources, Government of India.

viii) World Bank Canal Modernization Office

In 1978 it was proposed to construct a canal parallel to Upper Ganges Canal from Hardwar to Kanpur. The construction of this canal was started in 1984 from Hardwar. On completion the length of the canal would be about 1000 kilometer. This project is financed by the World Bank.

3.5.5 Commercial and industrial growth

i) Commercial growth

The first permanent market called *Main Bazaar* was built in 1850. This was constructed by the material left over from the building of Ganges Canal (Nevill 1921). *Main Bazaar* has two *chowks* (squares). After the establishment of railway station in 1880, the growth of the market extended along the station road connecting the *Anaj Mandi* (grain market) and the railway station. In 1947 the Amber Talab area shops and the *subzimandi* came into existence. A few shops were also constructed along the right bank of the canal for the rehabilitation of refugees.

As mentioned earlier, the establishment of Roorkee University and other institutions during 1847-1950 gave a great impetus to the commercial activities of the town. Because of these activities a new market with modern amenities came up in the Civil Lines. The growth of shopping arcades is now continuing along the new railway road, Dehradun bypass road and Roorkee-Hardwar highway.

ii) Industrial development

The establishment of Government Workshop in 1843, heralded industrial development in Roorkee. With the initiation of Thomason College of Civil Engineering in 1847 several new industries came in existence for manufacturing surveying, drawing and mathematical instruments.

Independence has inspired a quantum leap in the industrialization of Roorkee. A 'Quality Marketing Scheme' was introduced in 1954 to ensure adequate quality of the products. An industrial estate was set up in 1965 on a 10 acre plot near Ramnagar colony. By 1967 the estate had been fully developed and occupied.

Manufacture of drawing, surveying and mathematical instruments forms the most prominent of the industrial activity of Roorkee but is slowly giving way to units manufacturing electronic microprocessor-based instruments.

3.5.6 Other essential services

i) Police

Before the dawn of the present century, policing was the responsibility of the municipality. By 1907 it became a separate authority under the State government. Presently Roorkee is the head-quarter of Deputy Superintendent of Police, Roorkee Sub-division. Following is a list of *thanas/kotwalis* in the city:

Kotwali Roorkee	:	Civil Lines
Thana Purani Kotwali	:	Near Subzimandi
Thana Purani Tehsil	:	Purani Tehsil
Thana Gang Nahar	:	Ganeshpur
Thana Sot	:	Sot

ii) Post and telegraph office

Roorkee has the distinction of possessing the first ever post office with telegraph facilities in Saharanpur district under the Post Office Act 1866. Presently it has one general post office, 10 sub-post offices and one telegraph office. A FAX service has been started from 1990 by the Telegraph Office.

iii) Telephone exchange

Prior to 1939, Roorkee Telephone Exchange had just 25 connections. With the introduction of central battery system in 1939 this capacity increased two-fold. By 1966 the capacity had gone up to 200. The first automatic exchange with 300 lines came soon after and had a capacity of 500 by 1970. An automatic electronic exchange was introduced in 1990 with a capacity of 1500 lines.

Roorkee University has its own PABX telephone exchange. It was established in 1958 with a capacity of 720 lines on manual PABX system, 200 lines on TDBX system and 11 direct lines .

iv) Banks

Modern banking facilities were introduced in 1950 with the establishment of Punjab National Bank in Subhash Ganj. At present 10 public or private banks are operating in Roorkee in addition to the treasury, sub treasury and post offices. A list of banks is given below.

Punjab National Bank	:	Subhash Ganj
Canara Bank	:	Subhash Ganj Roorkee
Co-operative Bank	:	Subhash Ganj
State Bank of India	:	Civil Line
Central Bank of India	:	Rajputana
Indian Oversees Bank	:	Civil Line
Punjab and Sindh Bank	:	Civil Line
Union Bank of India	:	Civil Line
Oriental Bank of Commerce	:	Rampur Chungi
Bank of Baroda	:	Civil Line

3.6 PROBLEMS ASSOCIATED WITH DEVELOPMENT

The development of Roorkee has followed a haphazard pattern bereft of any long-term planning. This has led to the following major problems:

i) congested and unplanned settlement with narrow roads - this severely hampers traffic and very often creates traffic jams. The location of vegetable and grain market in the city core contributes to this problem;
ii) encroachment and its ineffective removal all along the roads;
iii) disparity in the potential of a site and its current level of utilization. For example the banks of the canal are being used as truck stands but they may be better utilized as recreational centres;
iv) dearth of well planned and managed open spaces in the city in general, especially the old city, with virtually no open spaces or vegetation;
v) improper drainage - several low-lying areas of Roorkee get flooded during rains;

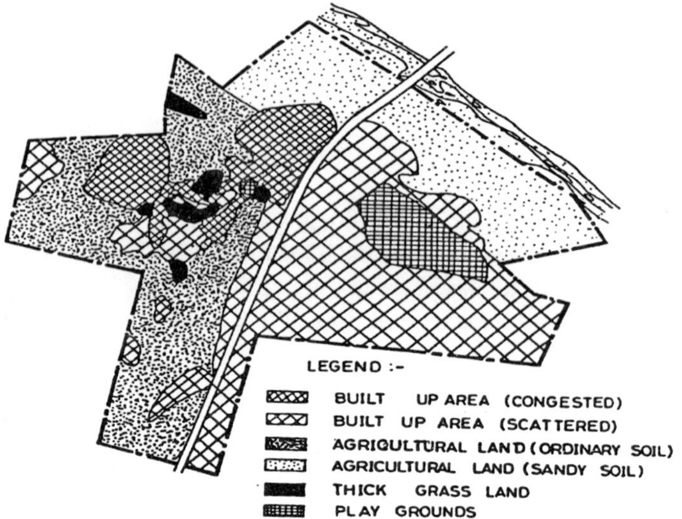

Fig. 3.6: Land-use pattern in Roorkee, 1962

vi) inadequate sewerage system - It does not cover the entire population of Roorkee;

vii) solid waste and sewage disposal sites created without a scientific basis;

viii) power demand not completely met - in summer,especially, power failures are long and often; and

ix) inadequate water supply - eventhkugh civic authorities claim that water is supplied round the clock at a brisk rate; in the peak hours and in summer proper head is not available in several areas resulting in a breakdown of supply.

3.7 THE DATA AND ITS SOURCES

3.7.1 Climatic parameters for the study area

i) Temperature and rainfall

Temperature and rainfall data of the test-case, Roorkee, (Table 3.10, 3.11) were compiled from the records of Indian Meteorological Department (IMD 1988 ;1994).

3.7.2 Land use data

The land use data was derived from aerial photographs (scale 1:25000) taken in 1962 (Figure 3.6). For 1990, the data was generated by the authors on the basis of land-use survey (Figure 3.7). The following categories of land use were identified and are given in Table 3.12.

TABLE 3.12 :
Land-use data

Description	1962		1991	
1 Built up area (congested)	0.844	10.40	1.435	17.68
2 Built up area (scattered)	2.899	35.71	4.486	55.28
3 Agricultural land (ordinary soil)	2.043	25.18	0.462	05.68
4 Agricultural land (sandy soil)	1.525	18.79	1.013	12.48
5 Thick grasslands	0.186	02.29	0.101	01.25
6 Playgrounds	0.462	05.68	0.462	05.68
7 Upper Ganges Canal	0.158	01.95		0.158
	01.95			
Total	8.117	100.00	8.117	100.00

(SOURCES : Aerial Photographs of 1962 & land use survey for 1991)

BUILT UP AREA (CONGESTED) : it contains the area of city core having almost no vegetation like Mohalla Rajputana.

BUILT UP AREA (SCATTERED) :it contains the area of Roorkee University and Bengal Engineers Group and Head quarter which have an appreciable concentration of vegetation.

AGRICULTURAL LAND (ORDINARY SOIL) : grasslands and agricultural fields except in the vicinity of river Solani are included in this category.

AGRICULTURAL LAND (SANDY SOIL) : agricultural fields situated in the vicinity of Solani river are included in this category because of appreciably different characteristics of the soil.

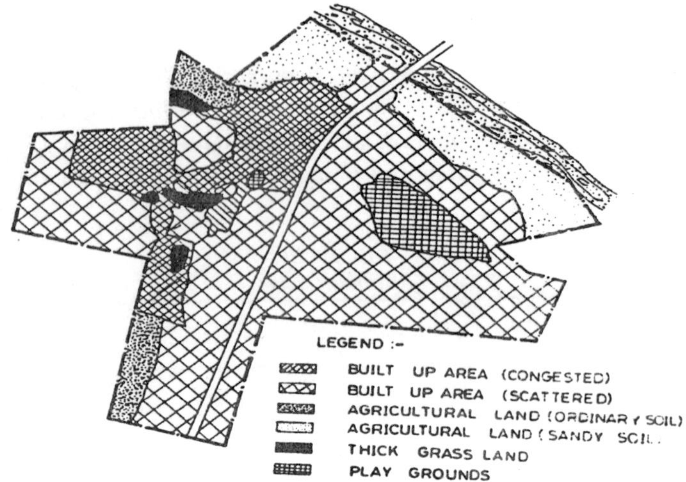

Fig. 3.7: Land-use pattern in Roorkee, 1990

THICK GRASSLAND : it contains all the gardens and thick areas covered with dense vegetation.

PLAYGROUNDS : Nehru stadium, Shastri stadium, Military stadium and other playgrounds are included in this category.

3.7.3 Water resources data

i) Water levels

Groundwater levels have been recorded since 1986 at Department of Hydrology, University of Roorkee. As, before 1986, no Hydrological station has been recording the levels within Roorkee town, the data for the hydrological stations surrounding the study area for the period 1971-1989 were taken from Ground Water Department (Table 3.13), Roorkee. These stations are also shown in Figure 3.8.

ii) Water quality data

Information pertaining to the quality of the ground water resources - which form the sole basis of water supply to the town of Roorkee

- is given in Table 3.14. Data for the preceding year is not available as none exists.

Table 3.13 : Ground water levels (m)

Station	Imali Kheda		Behri ki Saidabad		Beldi	
Reduced level	275.15		269.75		256.95	
Ground level	273.15		268.45		256.55	
Year	Pre	Post	Pre	Post	Pre	Post
1971	263.79	265.10	-	-	-	-
1972	263.54	265.12	-	-	-	-
1973	263.45	265.04	-	-	-	-
1974	263.65	264.83	-	-	-	-
1975	263.65	265.15	-	-	250.45	252.80
1976	263.78	263.78	-	-	251.26	253.12
1977	264.37	265.24	258.12	261.25	250.67	253.55
1978	263.75	265.97	261.23	266.70	251.30	254.07
1979	264.70	265.48	262.28	263.01	251.43	252.03
1980	264.06	265.09	260.00	263.08	250.57	252.59
1981	263.48	264.71	257.93	258.95	251.32	252.59
1982	263.40	264.42	260.14	261.05	251.50	252.58
1983	263.66	264.36	259.99	261.47	251.05	253.10
1984	262.94	264.30	259.93	261.45	250.70	253.64
1985	263.04	265.33	258.90	260.45	250.86	252.47
1986	263.50	263.53	259.67	260.63	251.15	252.47
1987	263.15	63.93	259.10	258.96	250.55	250.76
1988	261.92	264.12	Dry	259.17	249.66	253.78
1989	262.89	263.82	259.50	260.60	250.66	252.94
1990	261.90	263.12	259.20	260.50	249.55	253.70
1991	262.15	264.12	259.40	260.63	250.15	253.10
1992	263.04	265.20	259.20	261.47	251.26	254.05
1993	264.70	260.30	260.30	262.30	251.43	253.10
1994	263.25	263.95	259.23	260.17	250.55	253.50

Pre : Premonsoon Post : Postmonsoon
(SOURCES : Department of Hydrology, University of Roorkee, & *Ground water department, Uttar pradesh)*

Table 3.13 contd...

Station	Roorkee (Rampur)		Nagala Imarti		Roorkee (D.O.H.)	
Reducedlevel	266.23		264.95		-	
Ground level	269.20		264.25		254.22	
Year	**Pre**	**Post**	**Pre**	**Post**	**Pre**	**Post**
1971	-	-	-	-	-	-
1972	-	-	252.28	252.87	-	-
1973	260.88	263.36	251.57	253.05	-	-
1974	261.00	262.47	252.16	253.05	-	-
1975	259.78	262.18	251.02	253.75	-	-
1976	259.22	263.20	250.90	251.18	-	-
1977	259.67	261.90	250.63	260.75	-	-
1978	260.14	262.80	250.60	251.90	-	-
1979	258.85	261.10	-	-	-	-
1980	259.50	261.98	250.61	250.78	-	-
1981	259.84	261.17	250.49	250.73	-	-
1982	259.97	261.36	250.46	250.65	-	-
1983	259.73	261.74	250.17	250.61	-	-
1984	260.73	263.55	250.54	250.85	-	-
1985	259.61	263.54	250.22	250.48	-	-
1986	261.41	262.13	250.15	250.18	249.65	251.58
1987	259.59	259.95	249.68	249.45	249.29	250.57
1988	258.93	262.93	249.71	249.82	249.01	251.84
1989	259.89	263.16	249.86	250.39	250.33	252.24
1990	258.14	262.24	250.12	251.20	250.71	252.52
1991	259.74	263.23	251.22	250.25	249.35	251.25
1992	260.10	262.20	249.95	250.10	250.11	251.73
1993	258.93	263.85	249.75	250.48	250.44	252.84
1994	261.00	263.13	250.25	251.23	250.75	251.95

3.7.4 Demographic and socio-economic data

The demographic and socio-economic data comprising of population (Table 3.15), houses and households (Table 3.16), literacy (Table 3.17), and occupational pattern (Table 3.18) were culled from the Census Reports (DCH 1951, 1961, 1971 and 1981). The data for 1991 was taken from the Municipal Board, Roorkee.

i) Occupational structure

The occupation was defined as follows :

CULTIVATOR - persons who are farming on their own fields and cultivate themselves.

AGRICULTURAL LABOUR - persons engaged in agricultural activity on the basis of daily wages.

HOUSEHOLD INDUSTRY - workers engaged in manufacturing, processing, servicing, and repair works at household (cottage) level.

OTHER WORKERS - persons not included in above categories and engaged in trade, commerce transportation, construction, government offices and social service.

ii) Ward or mohalla-wise population

The ward-wise data (Table 3.19) was taken from Census Reports (DCH 1951, 1961, 1971 and 1981). The data for 1991 was taken from the Municipal Board, Roorkee. Ward wise maps of 1971, 1981 and 1991 are shown in Figures 3.9 and 3.10.

iii) Economic data

Even after persistent efforts, only very scanty data on collection of income and sales tax could be obtained from Income Tax and Sales Tax offices in Roorkee. As it was deemed improper to use such thin data for subsequent analysis, figures of receipt and expenditure obtained from Municipal Board, Roorkee, were instead utilized as indicator of economic growth. The data is summarized in Table 3.20.

3.7.5 Public health and infrastructural facilities

i) Birth and death data

Figures of birth and death (Table 3.21) were obtained from Health Division, Municipal Board, Roorkee.

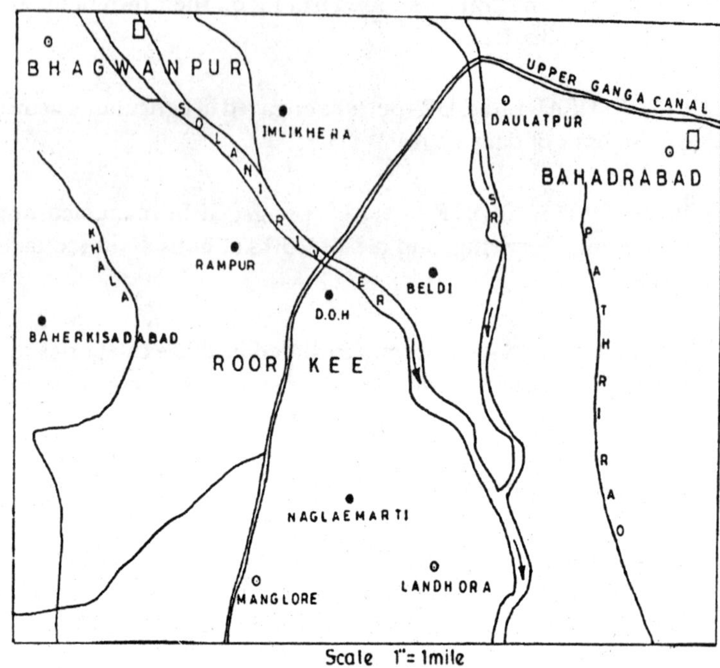

Fig. 3.8: Hydrological stations used in the study

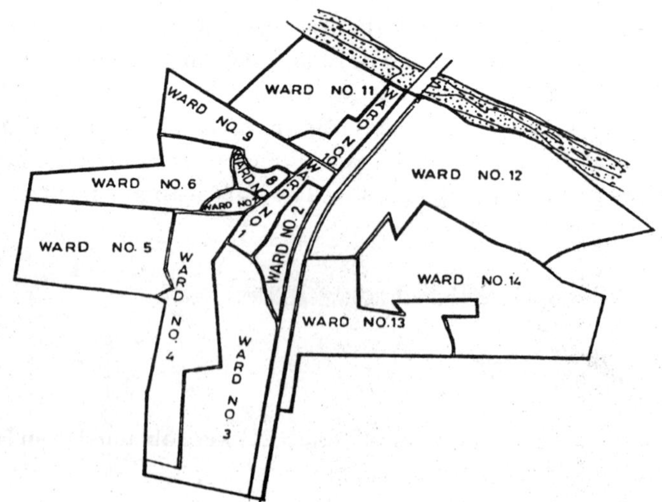

Fig. 3.9: Location of wards in Roorkee, 1971 & 1981

TABLE 3.14 :
Chemical analysis of ground water

Year	TDS	EC micro (ppm)	PH	So_4^- mho/cm	Cl^-	HCO_3^-	S_1^{+++}	Fe^{+++} Al^{+++}	Ca^+
				Chemical constituents in ppm					
1980	446	719	8.4	119	57	239	17	31	10
1989	322	480	7.8	13	7	273	5	3	32

Year	Contd.. Mg++	Na++	SAR	SI	Salinity	Quality
1980	31	19	0.67	-23.57	C_2S_1	Good
1989	14	31	1.13	-21.42	C_2S_1	Good

(SOURCE : Ground water department, Uttar Pradesh)

TABLE 3.15 :
Population of Roorkee

	Total			Municipal board			Cantonment board		
Year	Person	Male	Female	Person	Male	Female	Person	Male	Female
1901	17148	10028	7120	14197	8057	6140	2951	1971	980
1911	16584	10323	6261	13850	8336	5514	2734	1987	747
1921	16716	11015	5701	12246	7390	4856	4470	3625	845
1931	17476	10867	6609	13944	8266	5678	3532	2601	931
1941	27364	19088	8276	17334	10199	7135	10030	8889	1141
1951	33092	20109	12983	23239	13205	10034	9853	6904	2949
1961	45801	29154	16647	33651	19214	14437	12150	9940	2210
1971	62456	38054	24402	47561	26463	21098	14895	11591	3304
1981	79076	47528	31548	61851	33724	28127	17225	13804	3421
1991	100236	62834	41402	80236	42834	37402	20000	16000	4000

(SOURCES : Mitra, 1988; DCH,1951, 1961, 1971, 1981, 1991)

ii) Medical facilities

The data (Table 3.22) was generated by the authors from their survey.

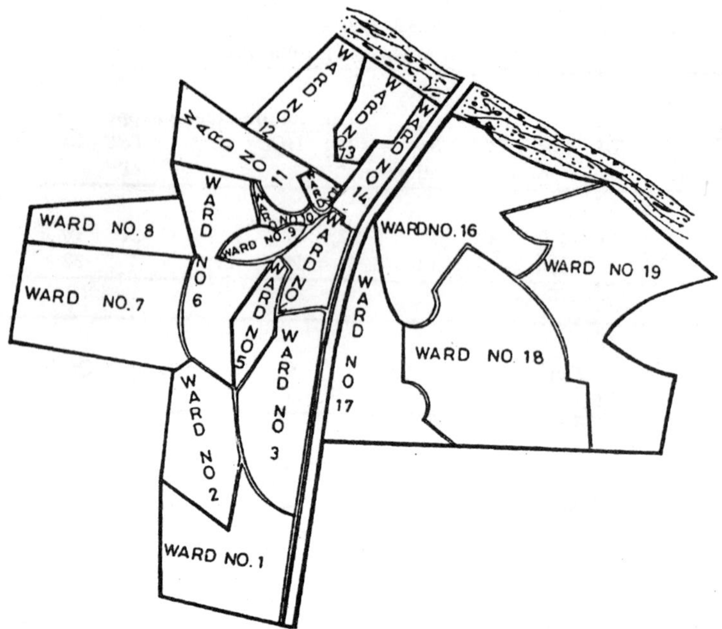

Fig. 3.10: Location of wards in Roorkee, 1991.

iii) Roads

The information on roads (Table 3.23) was culled from the census reports and records of Municipal Board, Roorkee.

iv) Electrification

The data related to power consumption - in terms of power connections (Table 3.24) were obtained from Utter Pradesh state Electricity Board and Municipal Board.

3.8 SELECTION AND DEFINITION OF INDICATORS EMPLOYED

Of the numerous parameters considered by us while analysing the developmental trends, 13 were identified for more detailed study. The methodology of doing it is explained in subsequent chapter (Section 4.4). The indicators are defined in the following sections.

TABLE 3.16 :
Houses and households

Year	Houses	Households
1951	-	-
1961	5170	6597
1971	8684	11910
1981	11193	11331
1991	14156	14285

(SOURCES : DCH 1951, 1961, 1971, 1981, 1991)

TABLE 3.17 :
Number of literates

Year	Male	Female	Total
1951	-	-	-
1961	12142	7072	19214
1971	17225	10601	27826
1981	25834	16177	42011
1991	32391	23920	56311

(SOURCES : DCH 1951, 1961, 1971, 1981, 1991)

TABLE 3.18 :
Occupational structure

Year	Total workers	Non-workers	Culti-vators	Agril. labour	H/hold industry	Other workers
1951	-	-	-	-	-	-
1961	9634	24017	222	21	305	9086
1971	12145	35416	229	39	204	11673
1981	15634	46217	284	119	385	14846
1991	20348	59888	394	172	628	19154

(SOURCES : DCH 1951, 1961, 1971, 1981, 1991)

TABLE 3.19 :
Ward or mohalla-wise population

Mohalla	1951	Mohl no.	1961	Ward no.	1971	1981	1991
Sot	1478	1	1026	1	3605	3480	4337
Satti	1466	2	182	2	3015	5311	5007
Qanungoyan	1184	3	2403	3	3637	6004	5900
Old Tehsil	774	4	1666	4	3663	4677	5334
Rajputana W	1931	5	1444	5	3159	4148	3452
Ambertalab W	1089	6	1798	6	3114	2647	5484
Maqtoolpuri	3252	7	4245	7	2867	2404	4756
Sheikhpuri	431	8	1125	8	3937	4140	2047
Ganeshpur	557	9	443	9	3161	4894	3244
Baaty Ganj	727	10	678	10	3432	3226	3993
Rajputana E	601	11	167	11	3367	5398	4369
Ambertalab E	368	12	3250	12	3335	2771	4685
P Dindayal	2297	13	1198	13	3865	2197	3323
Chowmandi	1045	14	1220	14	3818	10554	3374
Purwa Bali	497	15	2191	15	1092		
Civil Line	632	16	3516	16	5372		
Rly.station	2601	17	744	17	4184		
University	382	18	654	18	5713		
Malakpur	1554	19	838	19	4395		
Pathanpura	203	20	1055	20			
	161	21	3478	21			
	22	277	22				

(SOURCES : DCH 1951, 1961, 1971, 1981, 1991)

TABLE 3.20 :
Municipal receipts/expenditure (in 00 Rs)

Receipts

Year	Total Reciepts	Through taxes	Revenue	Govt. grant	Loan	Advance	Others
1951	7543	1484	554	429	5076	-	-
1961	9585	6317	1068	1224	976	-	-
1971	24018	5081	2708	3510	2985	616	9118
1981	26448	14368	8038	2840	1202	-	-
1991	92297	35790	21346	28068	7093	-	-

Expenditure

Year	Total expend	Genaral adminis	Public safety	Public health	Public work	Public instt.	Others
1951	9758	140	263	566	420	-	2750
1961	10028	196	562	1228	543	39	4496
1971	24965	1221	334	7438	2475	101	13196
1981	26418	4051	3034	14368	2461	-	2504
1991	92271	12424	3871	70036	-	311	56291

(SOURCES : DCH 1951, 1961, 1971, 1981, 1991)

TABLE 3.21 :
Births and deaths

Year	Death	Birth	Year	Death	Birth
1951	347	766	1973	200	811
1952	330	660	1974	215	700
1953	312	625	1975	185	660
1954	207	588	1976	216	772
1955	296	721	1977	171	595
1956	252	758	1978	173	674
1957	474	692	1979	183	572
1958	316	786	1980	201	647
1959	216	741	1981	201	638
1960	278	731	1982	194	726
1961	256	785	1983	189	631
1962	260	738	1984	214	666
1963	267	767	1985	251	675
1964	312	809	1986	205	849
1965	216	774	1987	292	1222
1966	198	725	1988	298	1438
1967	205	785	1989	311	1446
1968	192	787	1990	320	1250
1969	207	731	1991	305	1310
1970	216	708	1992	325	1427
1971	164	673	1993	320	1450
1972	180	685	1994	335	1495

(SOURCE : Municipal board, Roorkee)

TABLE 3.22 :
Medical facilities

Year hospitals	Number of doctors	Number of beds	Number of
1951	-	-	-
1961	6	4	69
1971	8	25	105
1981	6	42	96
1991	19*	61	500**

* Nursing homes considered as hospitals
** Beds of nursing homes are included.
(SOURCE : Based on survey)

TABLE 3.23 :
Road lengths (km)

Year	Total length	*Pukka* road	*Katchcha* road
1951	-	-	-
1961	-	-	-
1971	55.00	55.00	00.00
1981	73.83	71.00	02.83
1991	143.70	133.70	10.00

(SOURCES : DCH 1951, 1961, 1971, 1981, 1991)

TABLE 3.24 :
Electrification (no. of connections)

Year	Total	Domestic	Industrial	Commercial	Street light
1951	-	-	-	-	-
1961	2512	1800	170	-	572
1971	5039	2990	230	1032	787
1981	8482	6000	150	1000	1332
1991	18861	12000	300	4700	1861

(SOURCES : DCH 1951, 1961, 1971, 1981, 1991)

3.8.1 Environmental indicators

i) Climate

V1) *Temperature (max)*	= annual maximum temperature, C
V2) *Temperature (min)*	= annual minimum temperature, C

ii) Terrestrial

V3) *Land use*	= builtup area / total area

iii) Water resources

V4) *Water level (effect of withdrawal)*	= postmonsoon - premonsoon of next year, meters

3.8.2 Socio-economic indicators

i) Social environment

V5) Pop*ulation density*	= population / total area, person /sq.km
V6) *Birth : death ratio*	= births / deaths (in a year)
V7) *Literacy ratio*	= literate / total popualtion
V8) *Health ratio*	= number of doctors / 1000
V9) *Power* ava*ilability*	= numbr of domestic connections / total population

ii) Economy

V10) *Occupational structure*	= number of workers / total population
V11) *Financial receipts*	= total taxes and revenue, 1000 Rs
V12) *Transportation*	= length of roads, km
V13) *Expenditure*	= total annual expenditure,1000 Rs

4

INTRA - A NEW METHODOLOGY FOR SELECTION THE MOST INFLUENCIAL PARAMETERS FOR STUDY SO AS TO REDUCE THE COSTS OF EIA

4.1 INTRODUCTION

Theoretically, in any comprehensive EIA (Environmental Impact Assessment) one should study the impact of all possible indicators. But such an exercise may not only be too cumbersome but also costly and time-consuming. More important, such an exercise may not even be necessary because not all indicators would have a *detectable* or *significant* impact.

It is therefore desirable to seek a method by which one can not only assess the relative importance of the impacting indicators but, if possible, even draw up the hierarchical relationship among them. It is also equally important to establish which of the myriad indicators are 'stand alone' ones in their impacts, which ones serve as linkages, and which ones generate secondary and higher order impacts.

So far, there is not a single systematic study carriedout to achieve the above. When we explored the various techniques available for systems studies we found that Interpretive Structural Modelling (ISM) and *Matrice d'Impacts Croises - Multiplication Appliqnce a un Classement* or cross impact matrix-multiplication applied to classification (MICMAC), may be two of the basic techniques for us to build upon as they, conjunctively, provide the tools for developing not only hierarchical framework of the various indicators but also the pattern of interrelationships between them.

The techniques of Interpretive structural modelling (ISM) and MICMAC were introduced, separately, by Duperrin & Godet (1973) and Watson (1978) to deal with numerous variables that constitute any system and to bring to surface the role of otherwise low-key or 'hidden' variables in influencing system states. ISM-MICMAC also helps in developing hierarchical structures of the variables of the systems under study. Furthermore we have superimposed fuzzy logic on MICMAC to enable probabilities of interactions to be incorporated in the analysis of the system and the systems' responses to environmental impacts.

We have integrated the ISM and Fuzzy MICMAC methods to develop a new methodology INTRA (INTer-parameter Relationship Analysis) for EIA. When used in conjuction with other two methodologies described in subsequent chapters, INTRA enables a composite and cost-effective EIA of any system.

In this chapter a software package INTRA (INTer-parameter Relationship Analysis), capable of doing ISM analysis and FMICMAC, is developed. Using the package a case study of urbanization and its environmental impacts in the city of Roorkee has been conducted.

4.2 SOFTWARE PACKAGE INTRA

The package is designed in C language and works on DOS platform. The formulation used and their sequence is depicted in Figure 4.1. The analysis is conducted in three stages: i) ISM analysis; ii) development of Direct relationship matrix; and iii) FMICMAC analysis. The relevant data when fed through a data file in ISM analysis produces hierarchical levels of system indicators leading to a digraph; further the results of this analysis become input for further analysis. Second option develops a direct relationship matrix(DRM). Based on DRM a fuzzy direct relationship matrix is developed and being used as an input in third stage fuzzy analysis. Finally, FMICMAC analysis results in key indicators and their classifications. Some of the features of INTRA package are illustrated in Figures 4.2(a-e).

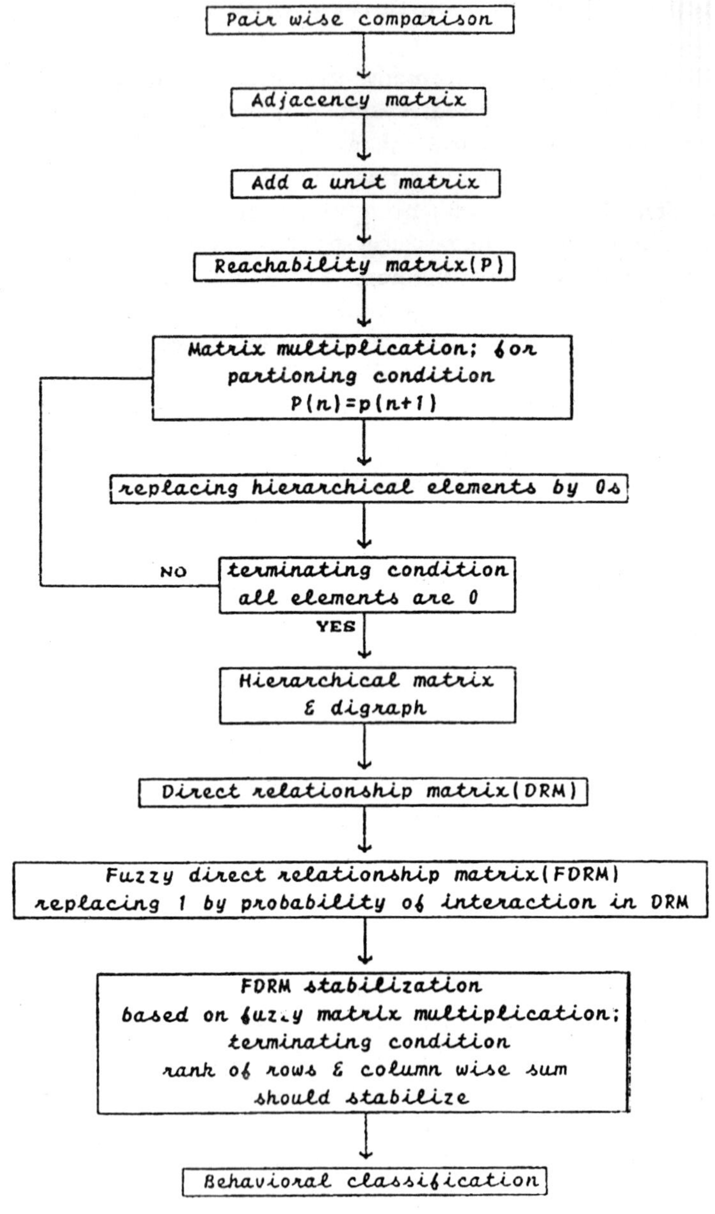

Figure 4.1: Methodological Flow diagram of INTRA

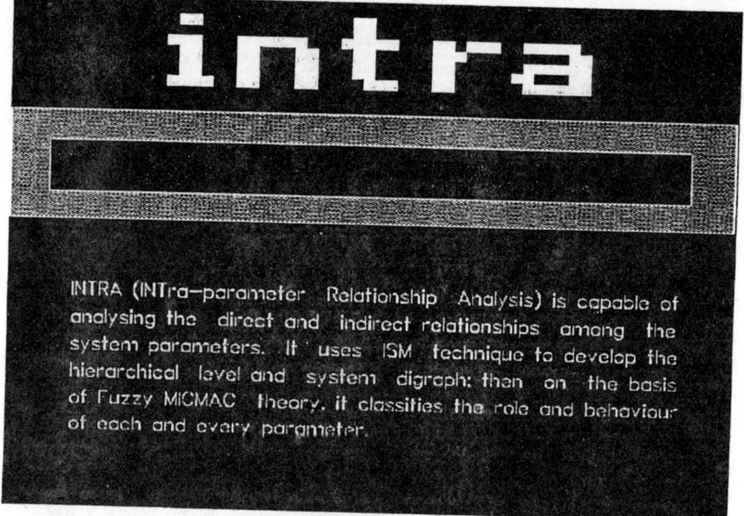

Figure 4.2a: Software INTRA

4.3 METHODOLOGIES INVOLVED IN INTRA

4.3.1 Interpretive structural modelling - An introduction

Interpretive Structural Modelling (ISM) is a computer-aided method for developing hierarchy of system indicators to represent graphically, the system structure. When the number of indicators that make any system is larger, it becomes difficult to consider all possible indicators; larger the number of indicators more tedious and complex is the process of assessing their interactions.

ISM is a method which enables one to handle the complexity of the system and resolve it into easily comprehendable form by working out the hierarchical arrangement of system indicators.

The main advantages of ISM are its easy computability and comprehensiveness. more elaboratively, the advantages of ISM are:

i) the process is systematic; the computer is programmed to consider all possible pair wise relations of system indicators, either directly from the responses of the participants or by transitive inference;

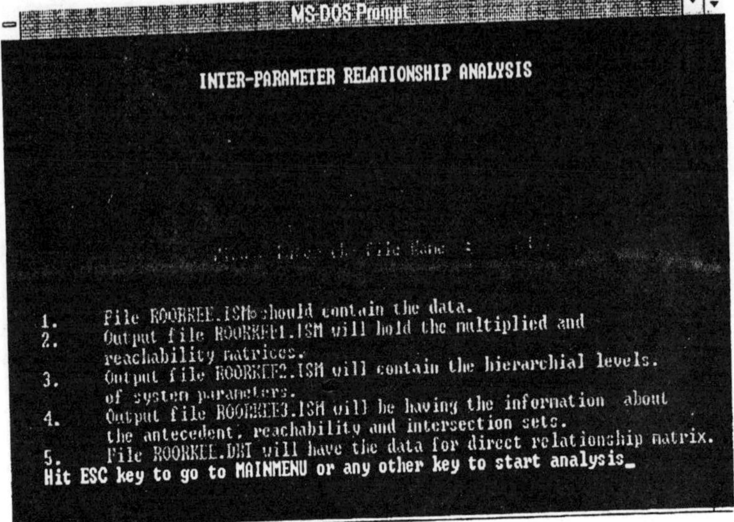

Figure 4.2b: Main menu and intermediate result files.

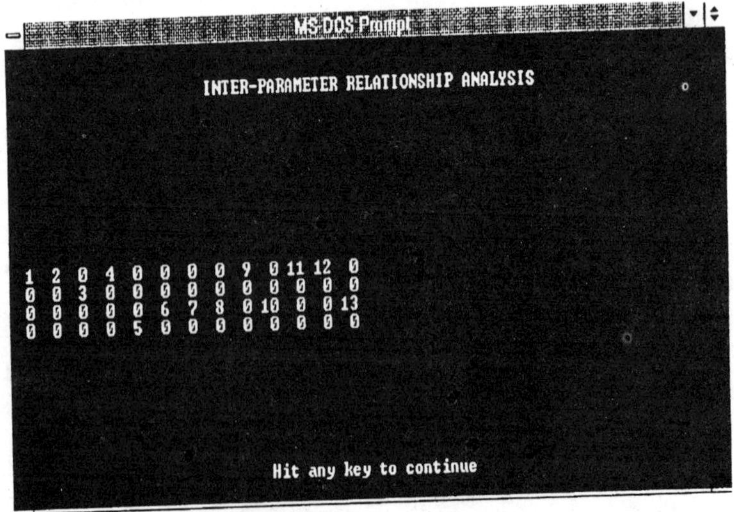

Figure 4.2c: Results of ISM analysis

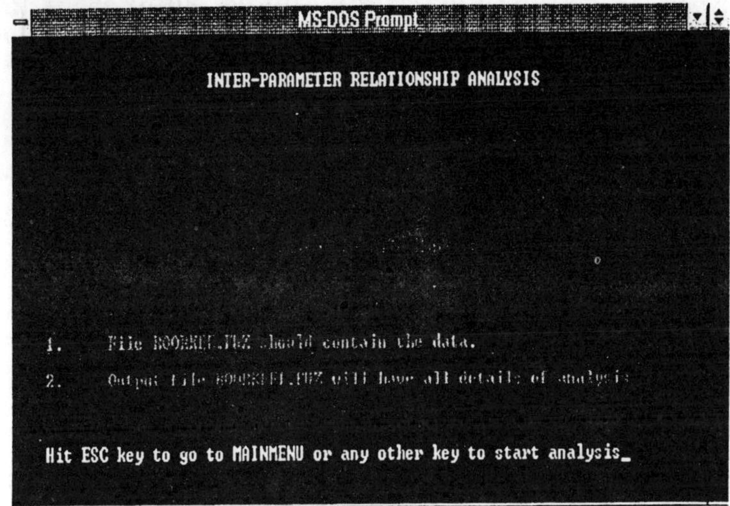

Figure 4.2d: FMICMAC analysis and output files

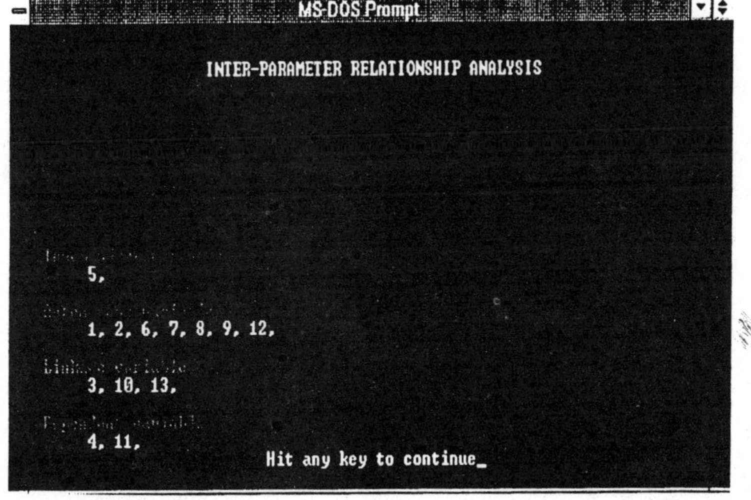

Figure 4.2e: Typical printouts of the results of fuzzy analysis

ii) the process is efficient; depending on the context, the use of transitive inference may reduce the number of the required relational queries by 50-80 percent;

iii) no thorough knowledge of the underlying process is required of the user; he/she simply must possess enough understanding of the object system to be able to respond to the series of relational queries generated by the computer;

iv) it produces a structured model or graphical representation of the original problem situation that can be communicated more effectively to others.

v) it enhances the quality of interdisciplinary and interpersonal communication within the context of the problem situation by focusing the attention of the user on one specific question at a time;

vi) it encourages issue analysis by allowing the user to explore the adequacy of a proposed list of systems indicators or issue statements for illuminating a specified situation;

vii) it serves as a learning tool by forcing the user to develop a deeper understanding of the meaning and significance of a specified indicator list and relation;

viii) it permits action or policy analysis by assisting the user in identifying particular areas for policy action which offer advantages or leverage in pursuing specified objectives.

Reachability and *transitive inference* are two basic concepts underlying in ISM process (Watson, 1978). These are elaborated below:

i) Reachability

The basic building block of the ISM algorithm is the *reachability matrices.* We may illustrate the concept with the help of a simple system given in Figure 4.3, and the *interaction* and *reachability* matrices constructed alongside the system.

D
|
A
B — C

Interaction

	A	B	C	D
A	-	0	0	1
B	1	-	0	0
C	1	0	-	0
D	0	0	0	-

Reachability

	A	B	C	D
A	-	0	0	1
B	1	-	0	1
C	1	0	-	1
D	0	0	0	-

Figure 4.3

Here the interaction matrix indicates whether or not there is a direct interaction between the row and column elements. On the other hand the reachability matrix indicates whether or not a column element can be *reached* from a row element along a continuous directed path (e.g., D is reachable from B). Whereas a unique reachability matrix is derivable for each interaction matrix, there are several possible interaction matrices for each reachability matrix. For example, the addition of a direct interaction between B and D would not alter the reachability matrix. As a result, the directed graph (digraph) which is constructed from the reachability matrix is the *minimum edge* representative of the system. i.e., that digraph which satisfied the conditions of reachability with the minimum number of interelement links.

It should also be noted that the digraph which is constructed from the reachability matrix is a hierarchical structure. In it there is no possibility for feedback from upper to lower levels in the structure.

ii) Transitive inference

An example of a transitive relationship is: if A is related to B and B is related to C, it may be inferred that A is related to C. The property of transitivity allows some of the cells of the reachability matrix to be filled by inference. For instance, in the previous example six cells can be filled by transitive inference: (B,C), (B,D), (C,B), (C,D), (D,B) and (D,C).

Through the use of reachability and transitive inference the ISM algorithm reduces the number of element pairs which must be examined to define system structure by 50-80 percent.

Fortunately, many important system relationships are transitive. These can be roughly classed into two types: ordering relationships and affective relationships. Ordering relationships are the ones which effect a strict hierarchical sequencing of the system indicators such as *more important than ... greater than ... more feasible than.* The use of the ISM for ordering relations is totally unambiguous. Example of affective relationships are relations such as: *affects .... influences ... causes ... supports .... aggravates .... contributes* to.

These seem to be the more interesting kinds of relationships for the kinds of problems with which Impact Assessment is concerned. However, as will be demonstrated, the use of ISM with such relationships is not entirely straightforward.

By assuming the transitivity of inter-connection and using computers, a reachability matrix is constructed. Optimized system paths can be represented through a digraph (directed graphs) incurred from reachability matrix. In a digraph, the indicators of a system are represented by the points of the graph and the existence of a particular relationship between elements is indicated by the presence of a directed line segment.

4.3.2. Basic steps involved in ISM - Conceptual framework

The steps in the ISM process are as follows

i) Defining a set of indicators (system components, objectives, problems, etc.) specific to a particular context which compose the system of interest.
ii) Defining a contextual relation which describes the interelement relationship to be explored (e.g., causes, affects, supports, aggravates, is more important than and so on).
iii) Conducting computer-aided ISM exercise during which the system structure (pattern of relationships between indicators) is systematically explored.
iv) Constructing the resulting directed graph (digraph) from the computer generated instruction.
v) Modifying the initial ISM digraph as necessary to achieve a satisfactory representation of the object system.

4.3.3 The ISM Methodology

i) Definition of indicators:

Indicators relevant to the given study are identified. For example in the study of the city of Roorkee the indicators identified by us are given in section 3.8.

ii) Developing a binary matrix called adjacency matrix:

The binary matrix represents the existence of relationships among indicators. Each indicator is compared with every other indicator; in other words pair-wise comparison of all indicators is made in order to identify a relationship for each pair. Whenever there is a relationship between two indicators, the corresponding element in the matrix is given a value 1, and 0 if there is no relationship.

TABLE 4.1. :
Adjacency Matrix.

	v1	v2	v3	v4	v5	v6	v7	v8	v9	v10	v11	v12	v13
v1	0	0	0	0	0	0	0	0	0	0	0	0	0
v2	0	0	0	0	0	0	0	0	0	0	0	0	0
v3	0	0	0	1	0	0	0	0	0	0	0	0	0
v4	0	0	0	0	0	0	0	0	0	0	0	0	0
v5	0	0	0	1	0	1	1	1	0	1	0	1	1
v6	0	0	0	0	0	0	0	1	0	0	0	0	1
v7	0	0	0	0	0	1	0	0	0	1	0	0	0
v8	0	0	0	0	0	1	0	0	0	0	0	0	1
v9	0	0	0	0	0	0	0	0	1	0	0	0	0
v10	0	0	1	1	0	0	1	0	0	0	1	0	0
v11	0	0	0	0	0	0	0	0	0	0	0	0	0
v12	0	0	0	0	0	0	0	0	0	0	0	0	0
v13	0	0	0	0	0	1	1	0	0	1	0	0	0

TABLE 4.2. :
Reachability Matrix.

	v1	v2	v3	v4	v5	v6	v7	v8	v9	v10	v11	v12	v13
v1	1	0	0	0	0	0	0	0	0	0	0	0	0
v2	0	1	0	0	0	0	0	0	0	0	0	0	0
v3	0	0	1	1	0	0	0	0	0	0	0	0	0
v4	0	0	0	1	0	0	0	0	0	0	0	0	0
v5	0	0	1	1	1	1	1	1	0	1	1	1	1
v6	0	0	1	1	0	1	1	1	0	1	1	0	1
v7	0	0	1	1	0	1	1	1	0	1	1	0	1
v8	0	0	1	1	0	1	1	1	0	1	1	0	1
v9	0	0	0	0	0	0	0	0	1	0	0	0	0
v10	0	0	1	1	0	1	1	1	0	1	1	0	1
v11	0	0	0	0	0	0	0	0	0	0	1	0	0
v12	0	0	0	0	0	0	0	0	0	0	0	1	0
v13	0	0	1	1	0	1	1	1	0	1	1	0	1

Table 4.1 shows the adjacency matrix for indicators 1 to 13. In this matrix, for example, *land use pattern*(V3) has a direct effect on the *water table*(V4), therefore, matrix element(V3,V4) is given a value 1. All such pairs which are effected by each other, are given a value 1; all others 0. All other elements are paired in this fashion.

iii) Obtaining reachability matrix *from adjacency matrix :*

Element a_i is reachable from a_j if a path can be traced from a_j to a_i. Here it is assumed that the transitivity relationship exists among indicators. That is, if a_i is related to a_j and a_j is related to a_k, then it is assumed that a_j is related to a_k. The adjacency matrix 'A' defines reachability having path length 1 and unit matrix 'I' defines reachability with path length '0' because in a unit matrix every indicator is a self-affecting indicator and does not affect any other indicator. Therefore, (A+I) defines reachability of all a_j to a_i having path lengths of 0 and 1. The reachability matrix 'P' is complete when the possible relationships through all paths are identified as '1'. This can be achieved when $P(n) = P(n+1)$ or $(A+I)^n = (A+I)^{n+1}$ (Vizaykumar, 1989). Therefore, the reachability matrix 'P' is defined as

$$P = (A+I)^n$$

Table 4.2 is the reachability matrix P obtained by using software INTRA.

iv) Partitioning the reachability matrix to obtain hierarchical matrix:

A series of partitions is made on the reachability matrix. These partitions are made to determine the hierarchy of the elements. For every element p_i in the reachability matrix, there may be some elements reachable from it; these elements constitute the reachability set $R_{(Pi)}$. Similarly, there may be some elements which can reach the element P_i constituting the antecedent set $A_{(Pj)}$. Therefore, the reachability set $R_{(Pi)}$ of the element P_i is the set of elements defined in the columns that contain 1 in row P_i. Similarly, the antecedent set $A_{(Pj)}$ of the element P_i is the set of elements defined in the rows which contain 1 in the column P_j. For example, in the reachability matrix (Table 4.2), in the first row all elements are 0 except in column 1. It means that this element can not reach or influence any other except itself. Therefore in this case reachability set $R_{(PV1)}$ = {1}. Similarly, in the first column, the digit 1 occurs only in the first row. It means that the element can be reached only by itself and no other elements can reach it. Therefore, the antecedent set of element 1 is given by $A_{(PV1)}$ = {1}. The intersection of the reachability set and the antecedent set, i.e., the common elements in both the sets results in $RA_{(Pi)}$ which is $R_{(Pi)}$ I $A_{(Pi)}$. That is, $RA_{(PV1)}$ = {1}.

Table 4.3 presents the reachability set, antecedent set and intersection set for all the indicators. The elements for which the reachability set and the intersection set are the same, are taken out to represent the first hierarchy or partition. According to Table 4.3, the indicators V1, V2, V4, V9, V11, V12 have the same reachability and intersection set, therefore, form the first hierarchy.

Hierarchy here means that no link is going out of this element, except a mutual link. However, one or more links may come to this element from other elements. In other words, it identifies a hierarchy similar to that of a vertical network in reverse order. Elements which will be at the bottom of a network are identified as the first level hierarchy in ISM. Unlike the networks, the links exist from lower level to higher level and also between the indicators at the same level.

In order to arrives at the second hierarchical level the rows and columns of the matrix containing elements of the first hierarchical level are set to zero. Table 4.4 shows the matrix with the elements of indicators V1, V2, V4, V9, V11, V12 eliminated.

The procedure is repeated with each subsequent hierarchical level until all elements are exhausted and reaches at the apex of the inverted pyramid. The hierarchical structure of the present example is given in Table 4.5.

TABLE 4.3. :
Reachability, antecedent and intersection sets.

	v1	v2	v3	v4	v5	v6	v7	v8	v9	v10	v11	v12	v13
	Reachability set												
v1	1	0	0	0	0	0	0	0	0	0	0	0	0
v2	0	2	0	0	0	0	0	0	0	0	0	0	0
v3	0	0	3	4	0	0	0	0	0	0	0	0	0
v4	0	0	0	4	0	0	0	0	0	0	0	0	0
v5	0	0	3	4	5	6	7	8	0	10	11	12	13
v6	0	0	3	4	0	6	7	8	0	10	11	0	13
v7	0	0	3	4	0	6	7	8	0	10	11	0	13
v8	0	0	3	4	0	6	7	8	0	10	11	0	13
v9	0	0	0	0	0	0	0	0	9	0	0	0	0
v10	0	0	3	4	0	6	7	8	0	10	11	0	13
v11	0	0	0	0	0	0	0	0	0	0	11	0	0
v12	0	0	0	0	0	0	0	0	0	0	0	12	0
v13	0	0	3	4	0	6	7	8	0	10	11	0	13
	Antecedent set												
v1	1	0	0	0	0	0	0	0	0	0	0	0	0
v2	0	2	0	0	0	0	0	0	0	0	0	0	0
v3	0	0	3	0	5	6	7	8	0	10	0	0	13
v4	0	0	3	4	5	6	7	8	0	10	0	0	13
v5	0	0	0	0	5	0	0	0	0	0	0	0	0
v6	0	0	0	0	5	6	7	8	0	10	0	0	13
v7	0	0	0	0	5	6	7	8	0	10	0	0	13
v8	0	0	0	0	5	6	7	8	0	10	0	0	13
v9	0	0	0	0	0	0	0	0	9	0	0	0	0
v10	0	0	0	0	5	6	7	8	0	10	0	0	13
v11	0	0	0	0	5	6	7	8	0	10	11	0	13
v12	0	0	0	0	5	0	0	0	0	0	0	12	0
v13	0	0	0	0	5	6	7	8	0	10	0	0	13
	Intersection set												
v1	1	0	0	0	0	0	0	0	0	0	0	0	0
v2	0	2	0	0	0	0	0	0	0	0	0	0	0
v3	0	0	3	0	0	0	0	0	0	0	0	0	0
v4	0	0	0	4	0	0	0	0	0	0	0	0	0
v5	0	0	0	0	5	0	0	0	0	0	0	0	0
v6	0	0	0	0	0	6	7	8	0	10	0	0	13
v7	0	0	0	0	0	6	7	8	0	10	0	0	13
v8	0	0	0	0	0	6	7	8	0	10	0	0	13
v9	0	0	0	0	0	0	0	0	9	0	0	0	0
v10	0	0	0	0	0	6	7	8	0	10	0	0	13
v11	0	0	0	0	0	0	0	0	0	0	11	0	0
v12	0	0	0	0	0	0	0	0	0	0	0	12	0
v13	0	0	0	0	0	6	7	8	0	10	0	0	13

v) Developing the digraph using the partitions

The structural model developed in the form of the hierarchical pyramid is represented as a digraph. In this the links between indicators are shown ; arrows indicating direction of the impact (Figure 4.4).

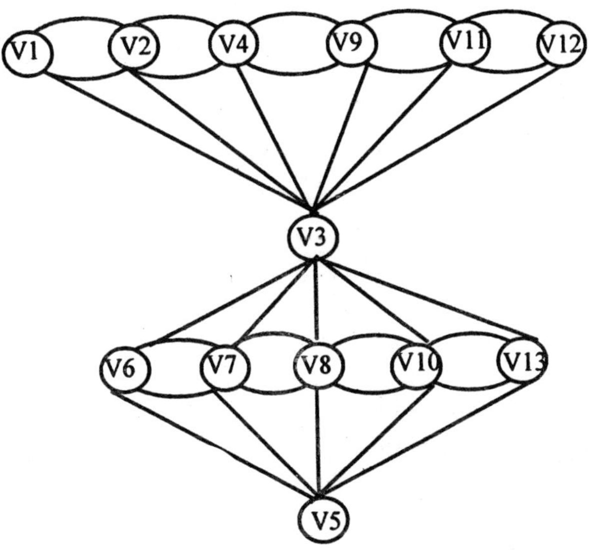

V1	: Maximum Temperature	V2	: Minimum Temperature
V3	: Land use	V4	: Water level
V5	: Population density	V6	: Birth death ration
V7	: Literacy ration	V8	: Health ratio
V9	: Power Availability	V10	: Occupational structure
V13	: Expenditure	V12	: Transportation

Fig. 4.4: Digraph for the case study of city of Roorkee

Austin and Burns (Austin, 1985) regard any digraph produced by ISM as a starting point from which alternative structural models can be obtained. However, they add that 'as for any model, an ISM is never perfect, however, there must be an adequate level of collective satisfaction in it'. In some cases minor modification of the initial ISM digraph is necessary to achieve a satisfactory representation of the system. This modification can be done with the collective wisdom of the EIA team fortified, if necessary, with the opinions of the experts in the area.

4.3.4 Development of fuzzy direct relationship matrix (FDRM)

The analysis can be further improved by considering the *possibility* of reachability in stead of the mere *consideration* of reachability used so far. The possibility of interaction can be defined by qualitative consideration on a 0-1 scale and given below:

Possibility of Reachability	NO	Negli-gible	LOW	Medium	High	Very High	Full
Numerical value	0	0.1	0.3	0.5	0.7	0.9	1.0

The possibility of reachability is superimposed on the direct relationship matrix (DRM) to obtain a fuzzy direct relationship matrix (FDRM). DRM is obtained by examining the direct relations between the indicators in the digraph, ignoring the transitivity and making diagonal entries 0. DRM and FDRM are given in Table 4.6.

4.3.5 FMICMAC Methodology

Examinations of direct relationships may reveal that indicators having strong direct impact can be suppressing hidden indicators, which at times may substantially influence the system under consideration (Saxena 1990b). Such indirect inter-relationship between indicators may have an impact on the system through influence chains and reaction loops, or feedback. The number of such chains and loops could be so large that it may be difficult to interpret them without the help of computers (Watson, 1978).

To analyse these inter-relationships and to study their role and behaviour, MICMAC method was intoduced by Duperrin and Godet (1973). The method enables study of the diffusion of impacts through reaction paths and loops for developing hierarchy of the indicators:

TABLE 4.4. :
First hierarchial elimination from the reachability matrix.

	v1	v2	v3	v4	v5	v6	v7	v8	v9	v10	v11	v12	v13
v1	0	0	0	0	0	0	0	0	0	0	0	0	0
v2	0	0	0	0	0	0	0	0	0	0	0	0	0
v3	0	0	1	0	0	0	0	0	0	0	0	0	0
v4	0	0	0	0	0	0	0	0	0	0	0	0	0
v5	0	0	1	0	1	1	1	1	0	1	0	0	1
v6	0	0	1	0	0	1	1	1	0	1	0	0	1
v7	0	0	1	0	0	1	1	1	0	1	0	0	1
v8	0	0	1	0	0	1	1	1	0	1	0	0	1
v9	0	0	0	0	0	0	0	0	0	0	0	0	0
v10	0	0	1	0	0	1	1	1	0	1	0	0	1
v11	0	0	0	0	0	0	0	0	0	0	0	0	0
v12	0	0	0	0	0	0	0	0	0	0	0	0	0
v13	0	0	1	0	0	1	1	1	0	1	0	0	1

TABLE 4.5. :
Hierarchial levels.

LEVEL-1	1	2	0	4	0	0	0	0	9	0	11	12	0
LEVEL-2	0	0	3	0	0	0	0	0	0	0	0	0	0
LEVEL-3	0	0	0	0	0	6	7	8	0	10	0	0	13
LEVEL-4	0	0	0	0	5	0	0	0	0	0	0	0	0

i) in order of their *driver power,* by taking into account the number of paths and loops of length 1, 2 .....n.... arising from each indicator; and

ii) in order of *dependence* by taking into account the number of paths and loops of length 1,2, ...n.... accruing to each indicator.

The driver power of the indicators in FMICMAC is evaluated by summing the entries of possibilities of interactions in the rows, and the dependence of the subelements is determined by summing the entries of possibilities of interactions in the columns.

i) The MICMAC principle

The MICMAC principle is based on the multiplication properties of matrices. If indicator i directly influences indicator k and if k directly influences indicator j, any change affecting indicator i can have repercussions on indicator j. There is an indirect connection between i and j.

Numerous indirect relationships of i a j type which exists in the structural matrix cannot be taken into account in a direct relationship approach. When the matrix is squared, second order relationships are revealed, such as i a j. Similarly, when the matrix is multiplied, 3,4,5 or n times, the number of influence paths (for influence loops) of the 3rd, 4th, 5th order interconnecting the indicators can be found.

TABLE 4.6. :
Binary & fuzzy direct relationship matrices.

Binary direct relationship matrix

	v1	v2	v3	v4	v5	v6	v7	v8	v9	v10	v11	v12	v13
v1	0	1	0	0	0	0	0	0	0	0	0	0	0
v2	1	0	0	1	0	0	0	0	0	0	0	0	0
v3	1	1	0	1	0	0	0	0	1	0	1	1	0
v4	0	1	0	0	0	0	0	0	1	0	0	0	0
v5	0	0	0	0	0	1	1	1	0	1	0	0	1
v6	0	0	1	0	0	0	1	0	0	0	0	0	0
v7	0	0	1	0	0	1	0	1	0	0	0	0	0
v8	0	0	1	0	0	0	1	0	0	1	0	0	0
v9	0	0	0	1	0	0	0	0	0	0	1	0	0
v10	0	0	1	0	0	0	0	1	0	0	0	0	1
v11	0	0	0	0	0	0	0	0	1	0	0	1	0
v12	0	0	0	0	0	0	0	0	0	0	1	0	0
v13	0	0	1	0	0	0	0	0	0	1	0	0	0

Fuzzy direct relationship matrix

	v1	v2	v3	v4	v5	v6	v7	v8	v9	v10	v11	v12	v13
	0	0	0	0	0	0	0	0	0	0	1	0	0
v1	0.0	0.1	0.0	0.0	0.1	0.0	0.0	0.0	0.0	0.0	0.0	0.0	0.3
v2	0.1	0.0	0.0	0.1	0.1	0.0	0.0	0.0	0.0	0.0	0.0	0.0	0.5
v3	0.3	0.3	0.0	0.7	0.0	0.0	0.0	0.0	0.3	0.0	0.5	0.3	0.0
v4	0.0	0.3	0.0	0.0	0.1	0.0	0.0	0.0	0.3	0.0	0.0	0.0	0.5
v5	0.0	0.0	0.0	0.0	0.0	0.7	0.5	0.7	0.0	0.7	0.0	0.0	0.9
v6	0.0	0.0	0.1	0.0	0.0	0.0	0.3	0.0	0.0	0.0	0.0	0.0	0.0
v7	0.0	0.0	0.3	0.0	0.0	0.5	0.0	0.5	0.0	0.0	0.0	0.0	0.0
v8	0.0	0.0	0.3	0.0	0.0	0.0	0.3	0.0	0.0	0.1	0.0	0.0	0.0
v9	0.0	0.0	0.0	0.1	0.3	0.0	0.0	0.0	0.0	0.0	0.3	0.0	0.5
v10	0.0	0.0	0.7	0.0	0.0	0.0	0.0	0.3	0.0	0.0	0.0	0.0	0.7
v11	0.0	0.0	0.0	0.0	0.3	0.0	0.0	0.0	0.3	0.0	0.0	0.1	0.1
v12	0.0	0.0	0.0	0.0	0.1	0.0	0.0	0.0	0.0	0.0	0.3	0.0	0.5
v13	0.0	0.0	0.3	0.0	0.0	0.0	0.0	0.0	0.0	0.7	0.0	0.0	0.0

Each time this process is repeated, a new hierarchy of indicators can be deduced. Their classification is based on the number of indirect actions (influences) they have on other indicators. When raised to a certain power, this hierarchy repeats in the next stage of multiplication (both in the hierarchy of column as well as in the row) and such a stage is considered as a stable stage and such matrix is called *stabilized indirect matrix.*

To the conventional MICMAC described above we have introduced fuzzy set theory to increase the former's sensitivity. Whereas MICMAC considers binary type of relationships, in fuzzy MICMAC an additional input of possibility of interaction between the elements is introduced. Eventhough FMICMAC is more sensitive than ordinary MICMAC analysis, the former continues to be useful in cases where enormous resources would be required to decide the possibility of interaction (Saxena, 1990c).

In FMICMAC analysis direct relationship matrix deduced from digraph- basic input to MICMAC - is enriched by incorporating in it the *possibility* of interactions. It is then called *fuzzy direct relationship matrix* and because an input to FMICMAC analysis; instead of using boolean multiplication of matrices to stabilize the ranks, fuzzy matrix multiplication is used.

Fuzzy matrix multiplication is basically a generalization of boolean matrix multiplication (Kandel, 1986). According to FST when two fuzzy matrices are being multiplied the product matrix will also be a fuzzy matrix. Multiplication follows the given rule:

$$AB = \max_k [\min (a_{ik}, b_{kj})]$$

where, $A=[a_{ik}]$ and $B=[b_{kj}]$ are two fuzzy matrices.

ii) Stabilization of fuzzy matrix

The fuzzy direct relationship matrix is taken as the base to start the process. The matrix is multiplied repeatedly until the hierarchies of the driver power and dependence stabilize. The multiplication process follows the principle of fuzzy matrix multiplications as described earlier. A stabilized matrix is shown in Table 4.7.

iii) Key Indicators

The indicators with the greatest driver power in the stabilized matrix are the key indicators. The key indicator that is nearest to the origin in the graph, represents the highest driver power.

iv) Behavioural classification of the system indicators

Based on the driver power and dependence worked out from stabilized matrix, the indicators are depicted in the driver-dependence graph in four sectors (Figure 4.5 & Table 4.8):

a) Sector I: Weak *driver power* and *weak dependent* indicators (points near the origin), a group of so-called *autonomous indicators.* These indicators are the factors relatively disconnected from the system; with which they only have few links, though these links could be strong.
b) Sector II: *Weak driver power* and *strongly dependent indicators.* These indicators are dependent indicators.
c) Sector III: *Strong driver power* and *strongly dependent linkages indicators.* These indicators should be studied even more carefully than the others. The linkage indicators are unstable. Any action on these indicators will have impact on others and feedback effect on themselves to amplify or support the initial pulse.
d) Sector IV: *Strong driver power* and *weak dependent indicators.* They condition the rest of the system and are called *independent indicators.*

4.4 APPLICATION OF INTRA TO STUDY OF URBANIZATION AND ITS ENVIRONMENTAL IMPACTS IN ROORKEE

As a prelude to the EIA a Delphi was conducted with the assistance of experts, to identify parameters or derivatives (henceforth referred as indicators) relevant to the study of Roorkee out of a set of over 150 possible ones. These 150 indicators - belong to 3 subsystems of environment and 2 of socio-economic - were analysed using INTRA;

the key parameters were cosen from each subsystem to study the urban system. This resulted in the short-listing of 13 indicators described under section 3.8.

Another round of Delphi was then conducted to determine which of the indicators influence which others - in other words *indicator pairing* was established. The adjacency matrix (section 4.3.3), which is a typical starting point of INTRA, is presented in Table 4.1.

TABLE 4.7. :
Stabilized fuzzy matrix (at level 5)

	v1	v2	v3	v4	v5	v6	v7	v8	v9	v10	v11	v12		Driver Power	Rank
v1	0.3	0.3	0.3	0.3	0.3	0.3	0.3	0.3	0.3	0.3	0.3	0.3	0.3	3.9	6
v2	0.3	0.3	0.5	0.3	0.3	0.3	0.3	0.3	0.3	0.3	0.3	0.3	0.5	4.3	5
v3	0.3	0.3	0.3	0.5	0.3	0.3	0.3	0.3	0.3	0.5	0.5	0.3	0.3	4.5	4
v4	0.3	0.3	0.5	0.3	0.3	0.3	0.3	0.3	0.3	0.3	0.3	0.3	0.5	4.3	5
v5	0.3	0.3	0.7	0.7	0.3	0.3	0.3	0.3	0.3	0.7	0.5	0.3	0.7	5.7	1
v6	0.3	0.3	0.3	0.3	0.3	0.3	0.3	0.3	0.3	0.3	0.3	0.3	0.3	3.9	6
v7	0.3	0.3	0.3	0.3	0.3	0.3	0.3	0.3	0.3	0.3	0.3	0.3	0.3	3.9	6
v8	0.3	0.3	0.3	0.3	0.3	0.3	0.3	0.3	0.3	0.3	0.3	0.3	0.3	3.9	6
v9	0.3	0.3	0.5	0.3	0.3	0.3	0.3	0.3	0.3	0.3	0.3	0.3	0.5	4.3	5
v10	0.3	0.3	0.7	0.3	0.3	0.3	0.3	0.3	0.3	0.3	0.3	0.3	0.7	4.7	3
v11	0.3	0.3	0.3	0.3	0.3	0.3	0.3	0.3	0.3	0.3	0.3	0.3	0.3	3.9	6
v12	0.3	0.3	0.5	0.3	0.3	0.3	0.3	0.3	0.3	0.3	0.3	0.3	0.5	4.3	5
v13	0.3	0.3	0.3	0.7	0.3	0.3	0.3	0.3	0.3	0.7	0.5	0.3	0.3	4.9	2
Dependence	3.9	3.9	5.5	4.9	3.9	3.9	3.9	3.9	3.9	4.9	4.5	3.9	5.5		
Rank	4	4	1	2	4	4	4	4	4	2	3	4	1		

TABLE 4.8 :
Classification of variables.

Independent variable	5,
Autonomous variable	1, 2, 6, 7, 8, 9, 12,
Linkage variable	3, 10, 13,
Dependant variable	4, 11,

4.4.1 Hierarchical analysis

The hierarchical matrix was fed to INTRA which identified the hierarchical levels of the indicators. A digraph was then drawn for interpretive structural model (Figure 4.4).

The digraph represents that indicator v5 i.e. *population density* (V5) which reflects the degree of urbanisation, is the main actor in the system under study. This indicator effects *birth death ratio*(V6); *literacy ratio*(V7), *health ratio*(V8), *occupational structure*(V10) and *expenditure*(V13) at second level. It means any change in population will affect all these second level indicators. The second level indicators are inter-connected too, therefore, if any change occurs in any of the indicator, it shall affect the entire chain. The second-level indicator most effected by the pattern of first-level indicators is *land-use pattern*(V3). Changes in *Land-use pattern* would cause reduction of vegetation cover and shrinkage in agricultural land; in turn effecting *temperatures*(V1,V2), *water level*(V4), *power availability*(V9), *financial receipts*(V11) and *transportation*(V12).

4.4.2 Development of binary direct relationship and fuzzy direct relationship matrices

On the basis of hierarchical matrix and the digraph, the direct relationship matrix was then developed. The possibility(likely magnitudes) of interactions between the indicators across the digraph were then introduced with the assistance of Delphi. This lead to fuzzy direct relationship matrix (FDRM).

4.4.3 Behavioural classification of indicators

Fuzzy matrix multiplication led to stabilization of the FDRM at multiplication level 5. The stabilized matrix is given in Table 4.7. Table 4.8 represents the classification of the system indicators. Based on the information derived from the FMICMAC stabilized matrix the indicators were classified (Figure 4.3) into four sectors; they are graphically presented in Figure 4.5.

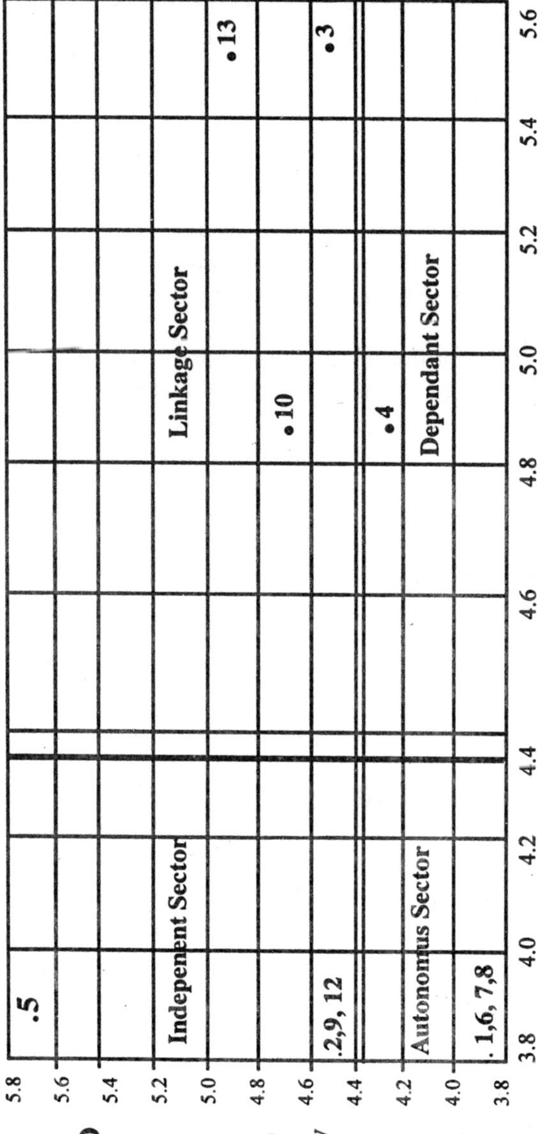

Fig. 4.5: Classification of indicators in different sectors as per their role in the environmental system

i) Key indicator analysis

The analysis reveals that indicator V5 i.e. *population density* - indicating the degree of urbanization, has the maximum driver power and is ranked it 1. This implies that *population density* is the key actor in the system under consideration and the entire system will be influenced by its behavior.

ii) Analysis of nature of indicators and their role

Independent indicators are the ones with high driver power. These indicators would strongly influence other indicators but shall not be influenced themselves. *Population density*(5) is an example.

It can be seen that autonomous indicators have relatively tenuous connection with the system, having only few links. *maximum temperature*(V1), *minimum temperature*(V2), *birth-death ratio*(V6), *literacy ratio*(V7), *health ratio*(V8), *power availability*(V9) and *transportation*(V12) come under this category.

Dependent indicators are totally dependant and influenced by the rest of the indicators. *Water levels*(V4) and *financial receipt*(V11) come in this category.

Linkage indicators are very unstable and should be studied carefully. *Land-use pattern*(V3), *occupational structure*(V10) and *expenditure*(V13) belong to the same category.

In summary the INTRA - based study of Roorkee indicates that the main actor impacting the environmental system of Roorkee is population density which is highest in hierarchy and has also the greatest driver power. The entire system is conditioned to it. However *autonomous indicators*, such as temperature and power availability are less influenced by the key actor. To understand the changes in this sector, it is good to analyze the indicator in view of regional and/or global changes. Land use pattern, occupational structure and expenditure-by-municipality are the results of the changes in *independent indicators.* These by-products, so-called *linkages indicators* bridge the gap between the independent and dependent indicators. For examples, changing population scenario will certainly change the land use pattern, therefore, it alters the water level (a *dependent indicator*); financial receipts too.

5

SMART-ALEC - A NEW SOFTWARE PACKAGE FOR STUDYING DEVELOPMENTAL TRENDS AND THEIR ENVIRONMENTAL IMPACTS

5.1 INTRODUCTION

Sustainable developmental planning requires in-depth analysis of past data. It also requires forecasting and scenario-construction to aid in decision-making (Abbasi, 1995a; 1995b).

The advent of microcomputers has made it possible for practically everyone to rapidly, accurately, and inexpensively process information, provided that appropriate software packages are available. Whereas a large number of general-purpose statistical packages are on sale in the international market, there are only a few which have been specifically designed for use in development planning.

This concern prompted us to develop SMART-ALEC (higher version of SMART) package, which is capable of identifying, quantifying and forecasting development-related trends for regional planning.

5.2 STRUCTURE OF SMART-ALEC

SMART-ALEC incorporates various statistical tests including several forecasting operations, summarized in Annexure to this

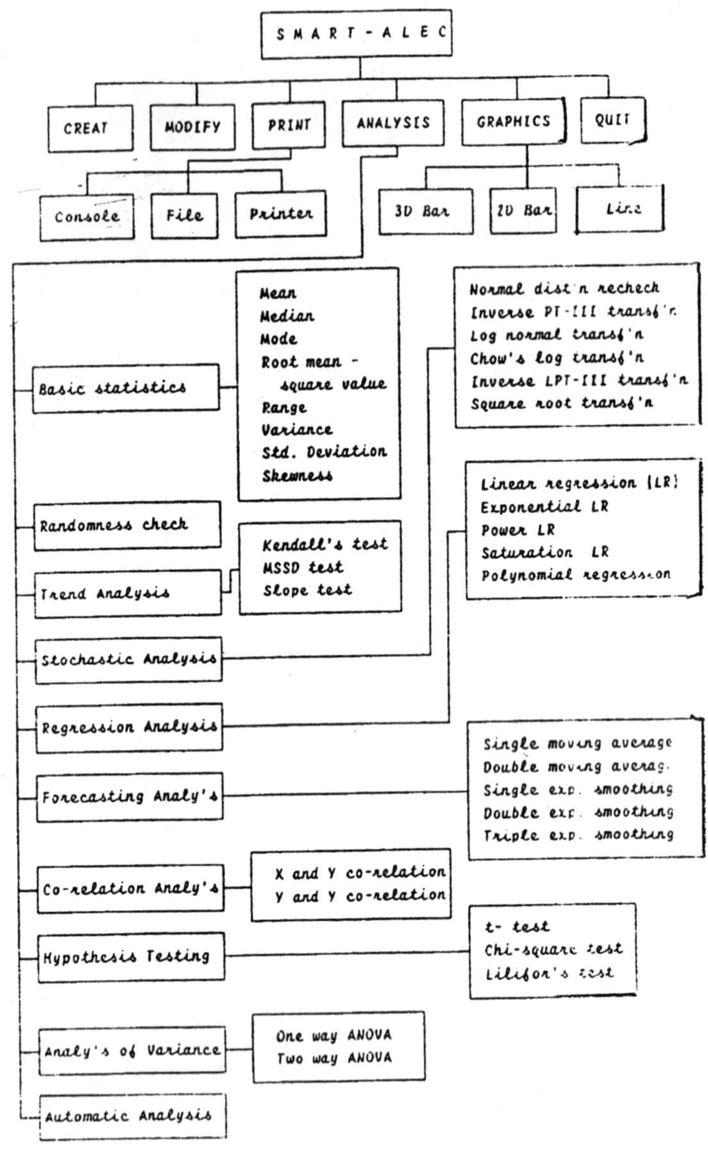

Fig. 5.1: Struture of SMART-ALEC

chapter. The superstructure of the package is presented in Figure 5.1.

The package is capable of execution in two modes- 'specific test' and 'automatic'. In the specific test mode the user can ask the package to execute only the test he/she desires. In the 'automatic' mode, the package would execute one by one all the tests (if necessary) leaving the user to assess for himself/herself which of the tests lead to significant results. Some of the features of SMART-ALEC are illustrated in Figures 5.2(a-f).

TABLE 5.1 :
% rise and fall in population; and population density, 1901-1991

TOTAL	% RISE IN	AREA	POPULATION	
YEAR	POPULATION	POPULATION	SQ.KM.	DENSITY
1901	17148	-	16.19	1059.17
1911	16584	-3.28	16.19	1024.33
1921	16716	0.795	16.19	1032.48
1931	17476	4.546	16.19	1079.43
1941	27364	56.58	16.19	1690.17
1951	33092	20.93	16.19	2043.97
1961	45801	38.40	16.19	2828.96
1971	62456	36.36	17.41	3587.36
1981	79076	26.61	17.41	4541.98
1991	100236	26.75	17.41	5757.38

The package is so designed that the print-outs of the results not only give the numerical values of the various analyses but also gives interpretation of the findings. Further the print-outs are in a form which are directly usable in the preparation of reports.

SMART-ALEC has been applied to the case study of Roorkee town. Data used in this case study is given in Chapter-III Following section discusses the analysis of the developmental trend and their environmental impacts due to increasing urbanisation of the town, using the same software.

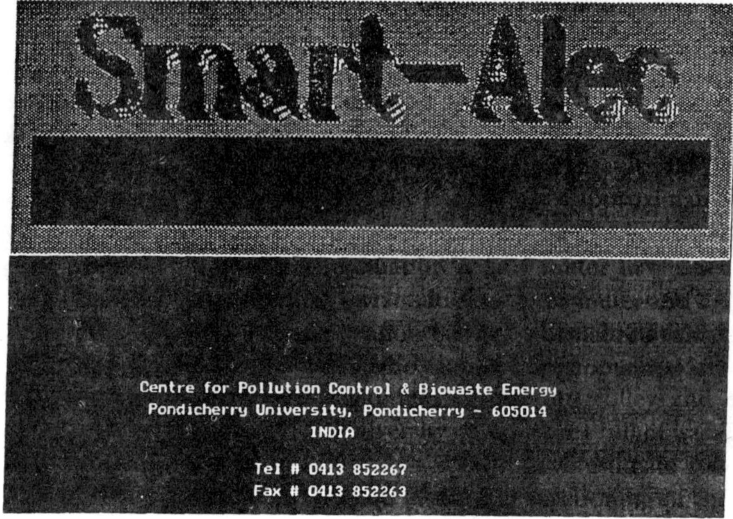

Fig. 5.2a: Software package SMART-LEC

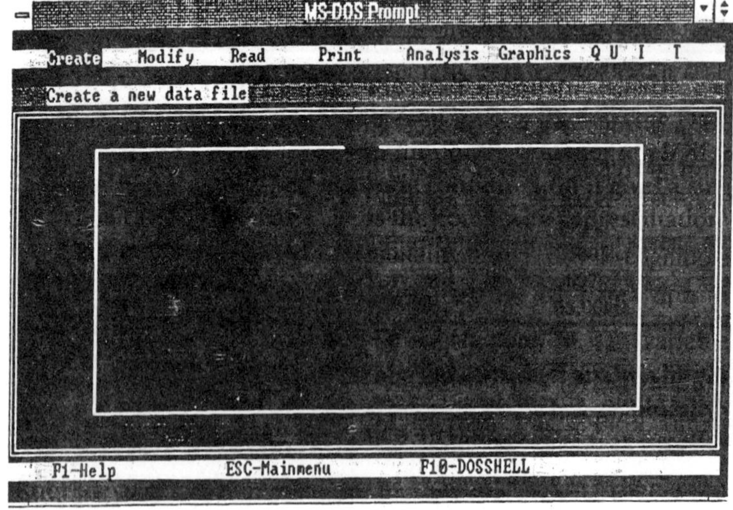

Fig. 5.2b: Main menu of SMART-ALEC

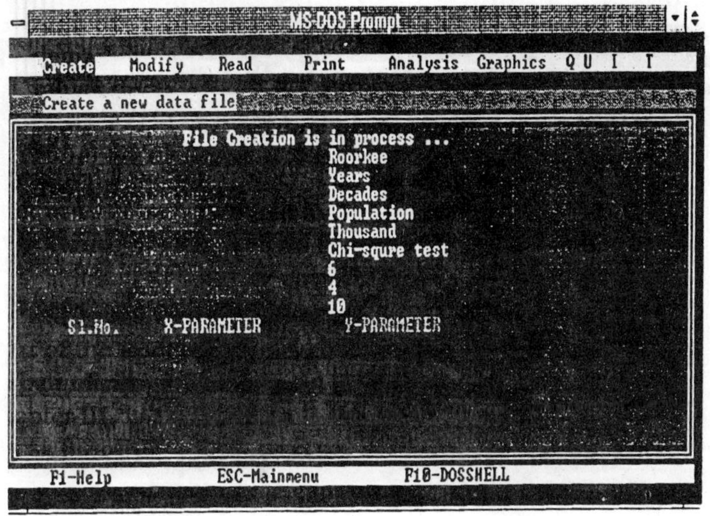

Fig. 5.2c: File creation in SMART-ALEC

5.3 DEVELOPMENTAL TRENDS

5.3.1 Urban structure

Prior to 1950, the settlement of Roorkee appeared to confirm to *concentric zone* theory or *open grained single nuclei* pattern, wherein all the major economic activities were concentrated at a focal point and the settlement grew around it (Jain, 1982). For some four decades the commercial activities incorporating the vegetable market, grain market and such other trading units in Roorkee were all concen trated at one point and people had settled concentrically around this point.

With time, some more markets and similar centres of economic growth came up in different localities of the town such as Ramnagar, Civil lines, Ganeshpur and Rampur Chungi, which served as nuclei for the growth of newer settlements. During the initial years of this phase of development, the urban structure was mare of an *open grained multiple nuclei* type, which gradually got

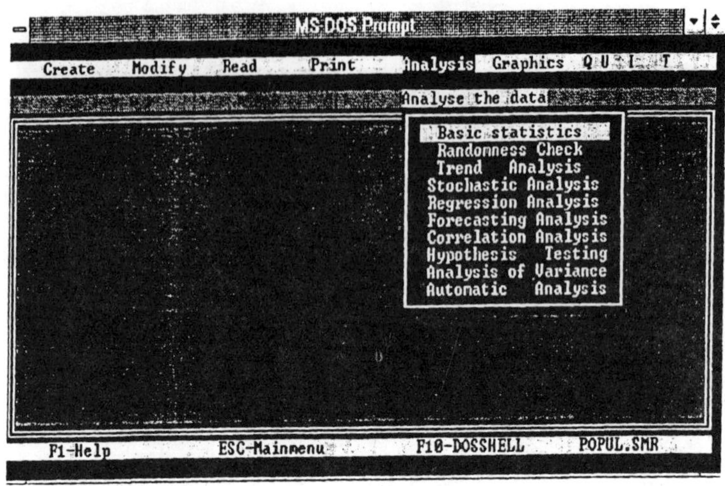

Fig. 5.2d: Options available in analysis menu

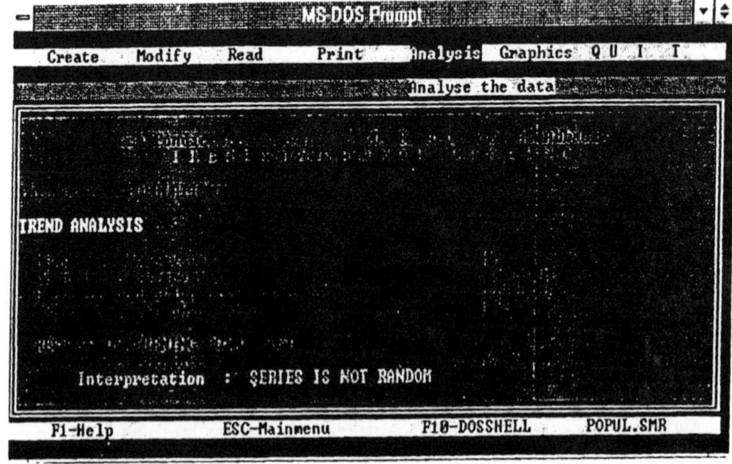

Fig. 5.2e: Typical output while operating in automatic mode

STATISTICAL MEASUREMENT FOR ASSESSING REGIONAL TRENDS AND LONG-TERM CONSEQUENCES

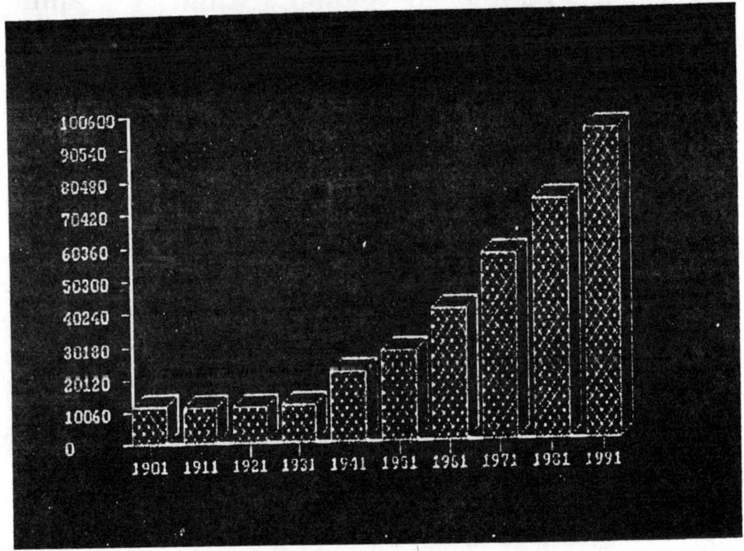

Fig. 5.2f: Typical graphical output of SMART-ALEC

transformed to a *compact grained multiple nuclei* pattern with a high rate of increase in population density. The growth pattern is shown in Figure 5.3.

5.3.2 Population

The demographical data for the period 1901-1991 is summarized in Figure 5.4. Figure 5.4 and table 5.1 presents decade-wise absolute population data as well as percentage change in population in each decade respective of the previous decade. There has been an overall rise of 485% in population; the maximum rise occurring in the 1940s and the minimum rise, 3.2%, during 1901-1911. Regression analysis indicates the statistically significant 'rising trend' ; the Mean Square Successive Difference Test typifies the trend as 'long-term' (Table 5.2).

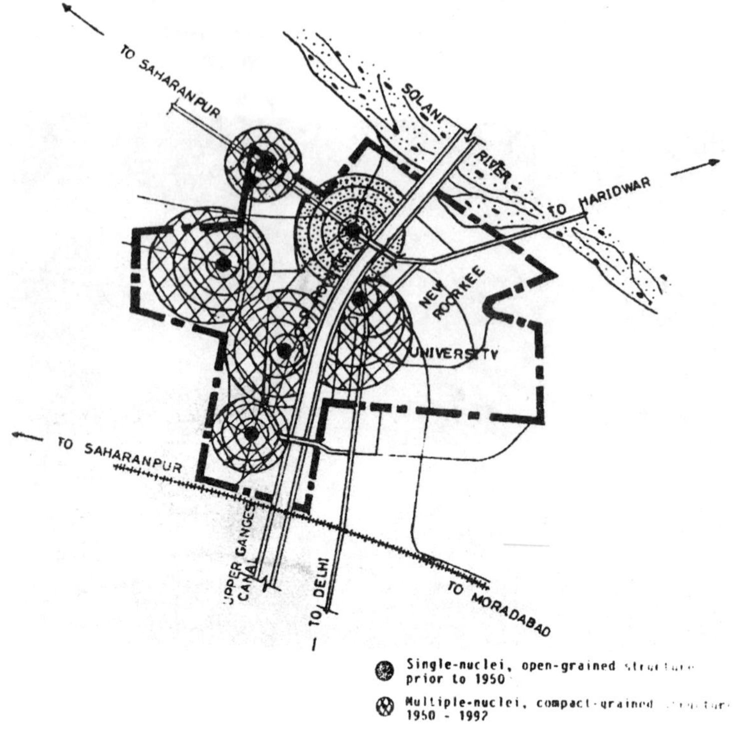

Fig. 5.3: Growth Patterns in Roorkee

Population density is seen to exhibit the same trend as that of population. However, the plot of percentage change shows an interesting variation in the sense that a moderately increasing trend manifested initially has been followed by a sudden sharp increase during 1931-1941 (upto 56%), followed by a drop in the subsequent decade and then a saturation phase persisting upto the present decade.

The overall population density of the town is quite high (5757 persons/sq.km.), comparable to that of two major Indian cities : Delhi (6319) and Chandigarh (5620). The density is also several times higher than the Indian average (267).

In terms of ward-wise distribution, there are wide fluctuations in population density - out of 14 wards comprising Roorkee the

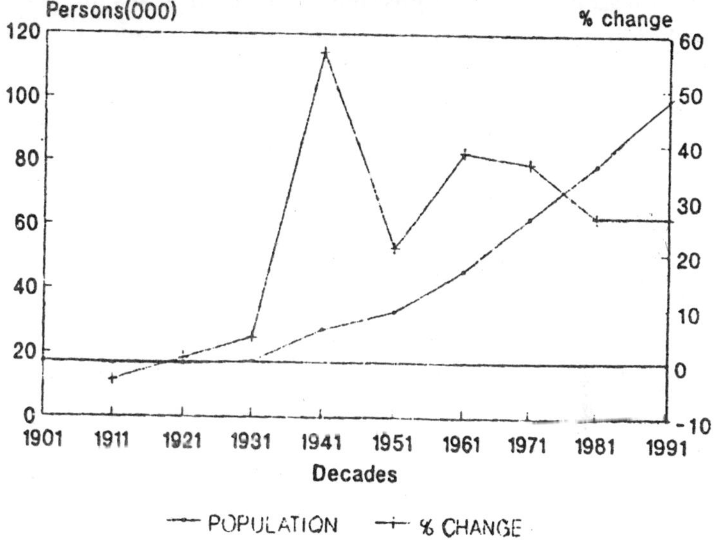

Fig. 5.4: Population of Roorkee, 1901-1991.

variation ranges from about 4000 persons/ sq.km. to 56000 persons/km (Figure 5.5 and Table 5.3). Results of ANOVA test (Table 5.3) run on this data show that the increase in population density has been significantly influenced by the spatial distribution as well as time domain in general in a statistical sense.

5.3.3 Sex ratio

The information concerning sex ratio (Table 5.4 and Figure 5.5) presents a surprisingly sharp decline of the order of about 40% during the initial four decades of this century. The data thereafter shows a stabilizing trend, yet the current value is far less than the national average of 927 females/1000 males. These results point towards the possibility of a higher female mortality rate.

5.3.4 Literacy ratio

The sex-wise distribution of the literate population is presented in Figure 5.7. There is a slow and steady trend of increasing female literacy over the last four decades while the progress in male literacy has been inconsistent. For both sexes the current level of literacy is significantly lower than the national average (62.86% in males and 39.42% in females).

5.3.5 Occupational structure

The occupational structure from the period 1961-1991 is presented in Figure 5.8. Although the number of total workers has increased from 9634 to 20348, the ratio of workers to population has steadily declined from 0.286 to 0.254. A classification of all the workers in terms of work place is also given in the Figure 5.8. Amongst the four categories, the category of 'other workers' (industrial and government workers) is predominant. As this category largely comprises of service class personnel, its predominance reflects the institutional fabric of the town. The growth in all other sectors such as household industry and cultivators has been quite moderate over the years.

5.3.6 Birth:death ratio

The figures of births, deaths and birth:death ratios are presented in Figure 5.9 and Table 5.5. The regression line for the birth:death ratio is also presented in this figure. The results demonstrate a statistically significant decreasing trend in the instances of death and an significant increasing trend in the birth:death ratio (Table 5.6). In physical terms, an increase of over 100% has been observed during the last four decades. These figures are consistent with the rising trend in population. These also indicate an overall improvement in the living conditions (specifically with respect to nutritional status) and access to better medical facilities in Roorkee.

5.3.7 Medical facilities

Medical facilities in Roorkee have received a tremendous boost during the last decade as demonstrated in Figure 5.10. There is a consistent rise in the numerical strength of two major indicators of medical facilities - number of doctors and number of beds. The steepest rise has occurred during the last decade due to the establishment of many private nursing homes and maternity centres concommittent with influx of specialists. The absence of any epidemic since 1911 has also contributed to the healthy trend.

TABLE 5.2 :
Trend and forecasting analysis of population

SMART-ALEC

(c) Pondicherry University
TRENDANALYSIS AND FORECASTING
Parameter :POPULATION
TREND ANALYSIS

Number of observations	=	10
Mean of 10 observations	=	41594.90
Standerd deviation of 10 obsevations	=	29805.26
Skewness of 10 observartions	=	1.05

RESULTS OF TURNING POINT TEST

Reduce variate Z	=	-2.76

Interpretation : SERIES IS NOT RANDOM

RESULT OF KENDALL'S CO-RELATION TEST

Reduce variate Z	=	3.67

Interpretation : RISING TREND EXISTS

SLOPE SIGNIFICANT TEST

Test statistic	=	6.95
Degree of Freedom	=	8

RESULT OF MEAN SUCCESSIVE DIFFERENCE TEST

Test statistic	=	-0.03

Interpretation : TREND PERSIST OVER A LONG TERM

FORECASTING EMPLOYING REGRESSION ANALYSIS 4 ORDER POLYNOMIAL REGRESSION

S.No.	Year Decade (X)	Population Persons (Y)	value regression eqn (Yr)	based on Y-Yr
1	1901	17148.00	20536.12	-3388.1:
9	1911	16584.00	16526.48	57.5:
i	1921	16716.00	15674.18	1041.8:
4	1931	17476.00	18031.97	-555.9:
5	1941	27364.00	23662.63	3701.3
6	1951	33092.00	32626.95	d65.0:
7	1961	45BOl.O0	44979.69	821.3
8	1971	62456.00	60793.64	1662.3.
9	19Sl	79076.00	BO117.61	-1041.6
10	1991	100236.00	103018.34	-2782.3
11	2001	0.00	129560.69	0.0
12	2011	0.00	159805.44	0.0

Goodness of fit	=	1.042862
Co-relation co-efficiant	=	1.000000

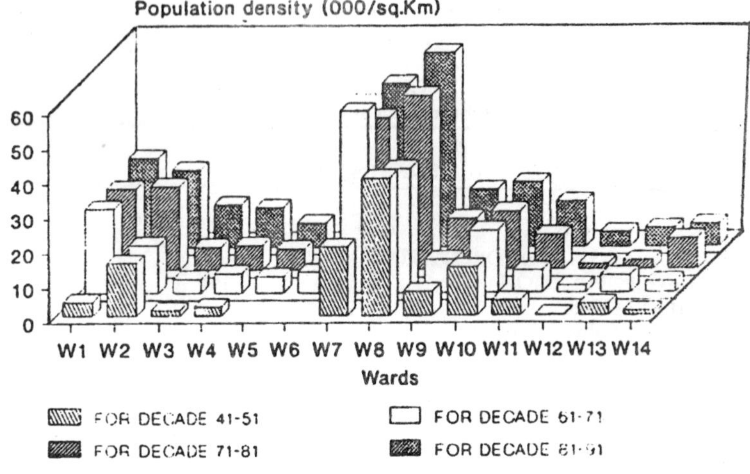

Fig. 5.5: WArd-wise population density, 1951-1991.

5.3.8 Municipal receipts

In the present study municipal receipts have been used as indicators to represent the economic condition of the region. Figure 5.11 demonstrates a consistent increase in the strength of these indicators with time; the highest values being attained during the last decade. Notable among the components of total municipal receipt are inflows through taxes and revenue which indicates the rising economic status of the residents of Roorkee.

5.3.8 Roads and electrification

The impact of growth of Roorkee is evidenced by an increase in the length of roadways, from 55 km (1971) to 143 km (1991). A similar rising trend is seen in the extent of electrification (Figure 5.12). There is a steeper rise in the commercial and domestic connections in the last decade in comparison to industrial and street lighting. This is consistent with the pattern of development of Roorkee which is predominantly educational-commercial; industrial development playing a secondary role.

TABLE 5.3 :
Ward wise population density and ANOVA table

SL.NO.	AREA (SQ.KM)	POPULATION DENSITY (sq/km) 1951	1971	1981	1991
WARD 1	0.1474	4077.340	24457.25	23609.22	25949.79
WARD 2	0.2184	15302.19	13804.94	24317.76	22500
WARD 3	0.9008	1677.397	4037.522	6665.186	12502.22
WARD 4	0.6551	2617.920	5591.512	7139.368	11625.70
WARD 5	0.6715	0	4701.414	6177.215	7082.650
WARD 6	0.5187	0	6003.470	5103.142	9232.697
WARD 7	0.0546	19908.42	52509.15	44029.30	47527.47
WARD 8	0.0819	39706.95	35860.80	50549.45	56678.87
WARD 9	0.3276	7017.704	9648.962	14938.94	16669.71
WARD 10	0.1911	13929.87	17959.18	16881.21	18655.15
WARD 11	0.5296	4229.607	6357.628	10192.59	13166.54
WARD 12	1.6488	220.7666	2022.683	1680.616	4349.830
WARD 13	0.7643	3403.113	5056.914	2874.525	5500.457
WARD 14	1.1793	1317.730	3237.513	8949.376	6519.121

Two Way Analysis of Variance

Source of variation	Sum of squares	Degree of freedom	Mean square	F ratio
Between Coulmns	815511680.00	3	271837216.00	12.58
Within Coulmns	9733036032.00	13	748695104.00	34.64
Sampling Error	842979200.00	39	21614852.00	
Total	11391526912.00	55		

5.4 IMPACT OF DEVELOPMENTAL TRENDS ON ENVIRONMENT

5.4.1 Impact on atmosphere

i) Temperature

The variations in the annual maximum and minimum temperatures during 1950-1990 are shown in Figure 5.13 along with linear trend lines. Although detailed statistical analysis (Tables 5.7 & 5.8)for both does not establish the trend to be significant

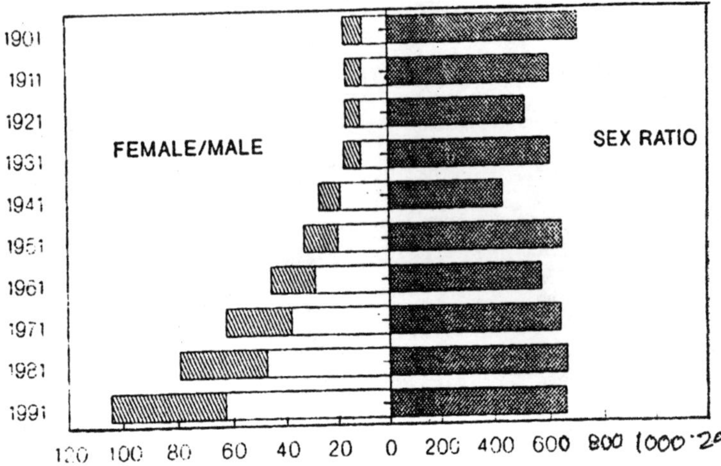

Fig. 5.6: Male/Female population & sex-ratio in Roorkee, 1991-1991

(confidence level < 90%), yet the trends of increase and decrease are clearly visible in the figure with respect to the maximum and minimum temperatures respectively.

TABLE 5.4 :
Sex ratio (Number of females/1000 males)

YEAR	TOTAL	MALE	FEMALE	SEX RATIO
1901	17148	10028	7120	710.01
1911	16584	10323	6261	606.50
1921	16716	11015	5701	517.56
1931	17476	10867	6609	608.17
1941	27364	19088	8276	433.57
1951	33092	20109	12983	645.63
1961	45801	29154	16647	571.00
1971	62456	38054	24402	641.24
1981	79076	47528	31548	663.77
1991	100236	62834	41402	658.91

The factor possibly responsible for an increase in the temperature is the conversion of agricultural land into urban land

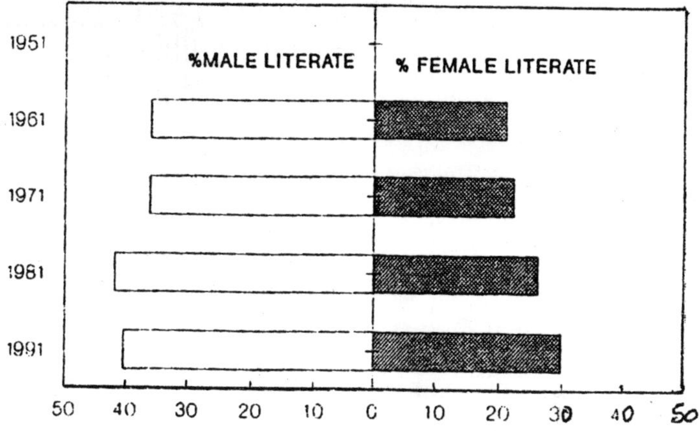

Fig. 5.7: Literacy in Roorkee. 1951-1991

and the rise in the level of related activities; the ratio of built-up area to the total area has nearly doubled in the past three decades (from 0.461 in 1962 to 0.729 in 1991). The immediate impact of clearing the land for buildings is reduction in vegetative cover and the consequent increase in radiation by the land surface. The subsequent redistribution of this energy generally results in lower evaporation loss and increase in sensible and soil heat fluxes. Both soil and air temperatures become accentuated, with high values and warmer conditions during the day time and, in most cases, marginally cooler conditions at night (Lawson 1986).

ii) Precipitation

The precipitation pattern during the last 94 years is presented in Figure 5.14. The trend line shows a visible decrease in annual rainfall but the trend is not yet statistically significant (Table 5.9), being below 90% confidence level. Precipitation being a phenomenon which is affected by several regional and global factors, beside local ones, the findings can not be conclusively attributed to any local factor but they are indicative of the adverse influence of deforestation as well as reduction in agricultural land in and around Roorkee.

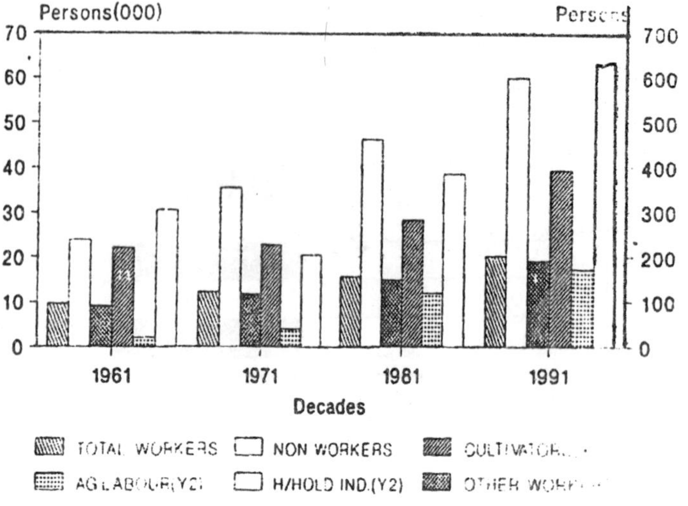

Fig. 5.8 Occupational Structure Roorkee, 1961-1991.

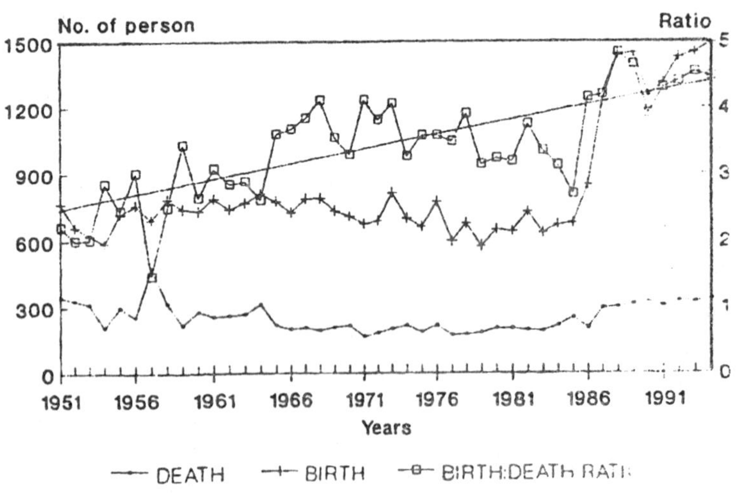

Fig. 5.9: Trend in births, deaths & ratio (with trend line), 1951-1994.

TABLE 5.5 :
Birth Death ratio, 1951-1994

Year	Death	Birth	Bd Ratio	Year	Death	Birth	Bd Ratio
1951	347	766	2.20	1973	200	811	4.05
1952	330	660	2.00	1974	215	700	3.25
1953	312	625	2.00	1975	185	660	3.56
1954	207	588	2.84	1976	216	772	3.57
1955	296	721	2.43	1977	171	595	3.47
1956	252	758	3.00	1978	173	674	3.89
1957	474	692	1.45	1979	183	572	3.12
1958	316	786	2.48	1980	201	647	3.21
1959	216	741	3.43	1981	201	638	3.17
1960	278	731	2.62	1982	194	726	3.74
1961	256	785	3.00	1983	189	631	3.33
1962	260	738	2.83	1984	214	666	3.11
1963	267	767	2.80	1985	251	675	2.68
1964	312	809	2.59	1986	205	849	4.14
1965	216	774	3.58	1987	292	1222	4.18
1966	198	725	3.66	1988	298	1438	4.82
1967	205	785	3.82	1989	311	1446	4.64
1968	192	787	4.09	1990	320	1250	3.90
1969	207	731	3.53	1991	305	1310	4.29
1970	216	708	3.27	1992	325	1427	4.39
1971	164	673	4.10	1993	320	1450	4.53
1972	180	685	3.80	1994	335	1495	4.46

iii) Air and noise pollution

So far no quantitative study have been conducted on the air and noise pollution in Roorkee. However increase in the noise and air pollution levels are being clearly felt. As Roorkee does not have any major industries, the deterioration in air quality and increase in noise levels are evidently caused by the vehicular traffic and the din created by human activity in the highly populated areas.

There is one more major source of air and noise pollution but its impact is only felt during April through June every year in certain localities. This is post-harvest treatment of wheat grains. In order to separate the grain from the straw the wheat crop is manually thrashed. This leads to the release of large blankets of

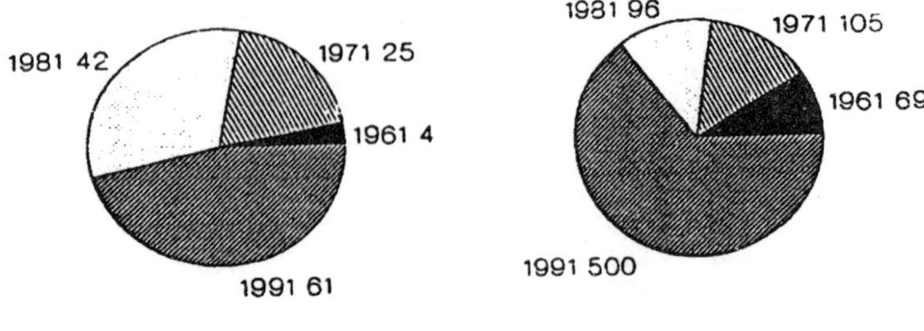

Fig. 5.10 : Medical facilities in Roorkee, 1961-1991.

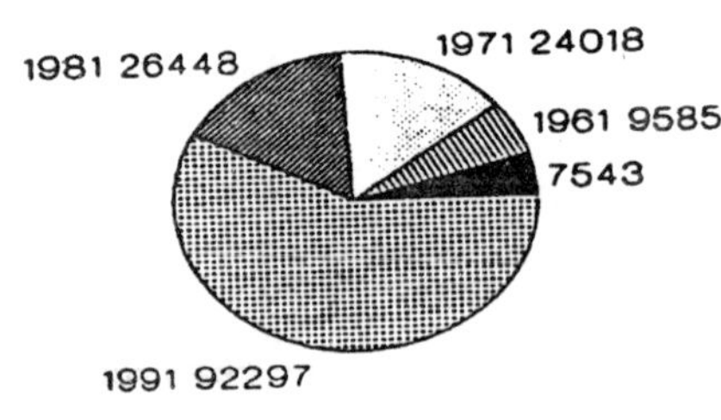

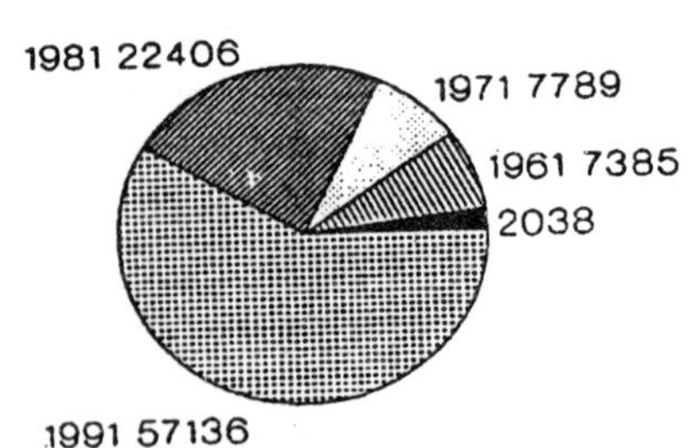

Fig. 5.11 : Financial Indicator, 1961-1991.

fine particulate matter which gets airborne and causes respiratory problems in downwind areas. The threshing action also creates an irritating cacophony.

TABLE 5.6 :
Tfend analysis of birth:death ratio

SMART-ALEC

(c) PondicherWy University i
T R E N D ANALYSIS AND F O R E C A S T I N G

Parameter :BIRTH-&-DEATH

TREND ANALYSIS

Number of observations	=	44
Mean of 44 observations	=	3.39
Standerd deviation of 44 obsevations	=	0.77
Skewness of 44 observartions	=	-0.33

RESULTS OF TURNING POINT TEST

Reduce variate Z	=	-0.73

Interpretation : SERIES IS RANDOM

RESULT OF KENDALL'S CO-RELATION TE5T

Reduce variate Z	=	5.26

Interpretation : RISING TREND EXISTS

SLOPE SIGNIFICANT TEST

Test statistic	=	7.58
Degree of Freedom	=	42

RESULT OF MEAN SUCCESSIVE DIFFERENCE TEST

Test statistic	=	-0.01

Interpretation : TREND PERSIST OVER A LONG TERM

STOCHASTIC ANALYSIS

CHOW'S LOGNORM~L TRANSFORMATION

Mean of the (transformed) series	=	1.197
Standeed deviation of the (transformed) series	=	0.224
Skewness of the (transformed) series	=	-1.030
Chi-square test statistics	=	2.091

Degree of freedom = 3

TABLE 5.7 :
Trend analysis of maximum temperature

SMART-ALEC

T R E N D ANALYSIS AND F O R E C A S T I N G

Parameter :TEMP(MAX)
TREND ANALYSIS

Number of observations	=	45
Mean of 45 observations	=	44.46
Standerd deviation of 45 obsevations	=	1.S4
Skewness of 45 observartions	=	-0.28

RESULTS OF TURNING POINT TEST

Reduce variate Z	=	-3.49

Interpretation : SERIES IS NOT RANDOM

RESULT OF KENDALL'S CO-RELATION TEST

Reduce variate Z	=	0.25

Interpretation : NO TREND EXISTS
SLOPE SIGNIFICANT TEST

Test statistic	=	0.93
Degree of Freedom	=	43

FORECASTING EMPLOYING REGRESSION ANALYSIS
4 ORDER POLYNOMIAL REGRESSION

S.No.	Year 1	Temperature Centigrade (X)	value based on regression eqn (Y)	Y-Yr (Yr)
1	1950	41.70	45.22	-3.52
2	1951	44.40	45.22	-0.82
3	1952	44.40	45.22	-0.82
4	1953	44.40	45.22	-0.82
–	–	–	–	–
–	–	–	–	–
44	1993	45.00	45.92	-0.92
45	1994	44.00	45.96	-1.96
46	1995	0.00	45.99	0.00
47	1996	0.00	46.03	0.00

Goodness of fit	=	0.021938
Co-relation co-efficiant	=	0.148114

TABLE 5.8 :
Trend analysis of maximum temperature

SMART—ALEC

(c) Pondicherry University
TREND ANALYSIS AND FORECASTING
Parameter : TEMP (MIN)

TREND ANALYSIS

Number of observations	=	45
Mean of 45 observations	=	2.18
Standard deviation of 45 observations	=	1.10
Skewness of 45 observations	=	0.23

RESULTS OF TURNING POINT TEST

Reduce variate Z	=	-3.13

Interpretation : SERIES IS NOT RANDOM

RESULT OF KENDALL'S CO-RELATION TEST

Reduce variate z	=	-1.64

Interpretation : NO TREND EXISTS

SLOPE SIGNIFICANT TEST

Test statistic	=	-1.39
Degree of Freedom	=	43

FORECASTING EMPLOYING REGRESSION ANALYSIS 4 ORDER POLYNOMIAL REGRESSION

S.No.	Year 1 (X)	Temperature Centigrade (Y)	value based on regression eqn (Yr)	Y-Yr
1	1950	2.20	3.70	-1.50
2	1951	3.80	3.67	0.13
3	1952	4.40	3.63	0.77
4	1953	2.80	3.60	-0.80
-	-	-	-	-
-	-	-	-	-
44	1993	2.30	2.95	-0.65
45	1994	1.60	2.95	-1.35
46	1995	0.00	2.95	0.00
47	1996	0.00	2.96	0.00

Goodness of fit	=	0.046547
Co-relation co-efficiant	=	0.215748

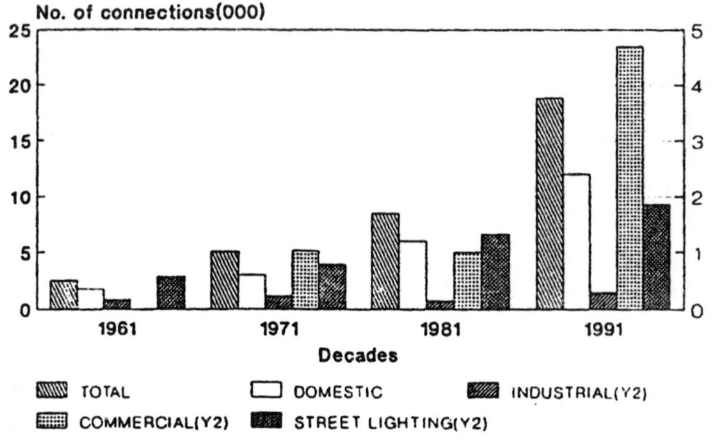

Fig. 5.12 : Rise in electrification in Roorkee, 1961-1991

5.4.2 Impact on terrestrial system

i) Land use

When a town is subjected to demographic pressure there is initially an increase in built-up area but the boundaries of the town being essentially limited, a saturation phase is soon reached. Further growth in population leads to vertical growth and congestion. Roorkee's core area is now congested and the problem is fast approaching alarming proportions.

The impact of this rapid urbanisation is seen in the changing land use pattern during the years 1961 through to 1991 (Figure 5.15). The percentage of built up area has increased from 45% (in 1961) to 72% (in 1991), causing a 27% decrease in the productive agricultural land of the town and its surroundings.

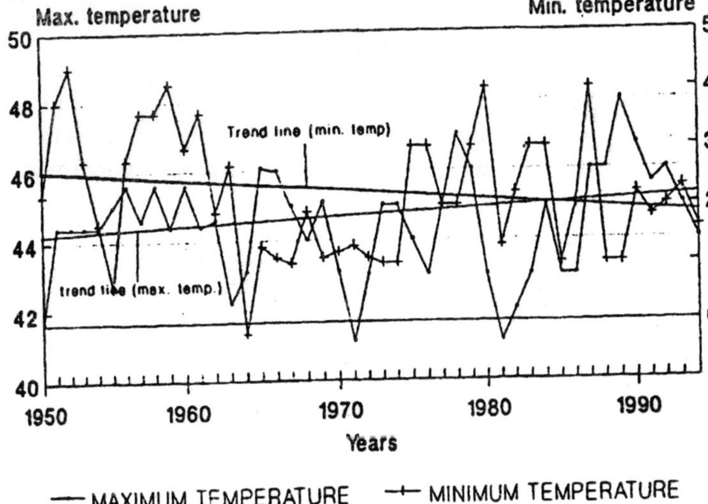

Fig. 5.13 :Pattern of changes in the yearly maximum and minimum temperatures (in centigrade) in Roorkee, 1950-1994

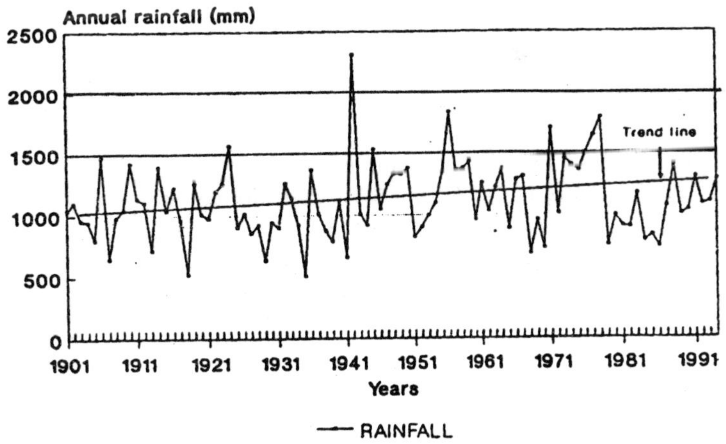

Fig. 5.14: Annual rainfall in Roorkee, 1901-1994

ii) Run off

The built-up area being mostly impervious, a shift towards increasing urbanisation is expected to cause a decrease in rainwater infiltration with a consequent increase in run-off. This in turn may lead to shorter hydrological peaking times, storm-water accumulation and flooding (Lazaro 1979).

The extent of impact of urbanisation on land-use can be assessed from the following calculation. Run-off was computed using Soil Conservation Service (SCS) method (SCS 1972, Soni 1986; Saeed 1987) for the land-use patterns of 1961 and 1991 for the same assumed rainfall intensity of 100 mm (Table 5.10), leading to figures of 399231.2 and 463019.5 cubic meters respectively. There is thus a 17% increase in run-off in 1991 compared to 1967.

5.4.3 Impact on water resources

i) Status of water table and withdrawal fluctuations

The trends in water table fluctuations, withdrawal effects and recharge effects are presented in Figure 5.16 (a-c) and Table 5.11for a hydrological station of the Ground Water Department (Government of Utter Pradesh), situated within the confines of Roorkee.

The figures reveal visibly decreasing trends but these are not statistically significant (Table 5.12; confidence level < 90%). The decreasing recharge rate is likely to be due to a combination of various factors: decrease in rainfall during 1975-1991, continuously increasing built-up area; and the gradually increasing withdrawal.

TABLE 5.9 :
Trend analysis of precipation data

SMART ALEC
(c) Pondicherry University
TREND ANALYSIS AND FORECASTING
Parameter : Precipation

TREND ANALYSIS		
Number of observations	=	94
Mean of 94 observations	=	1115.69
Standard deviation of 94 observations	=	301.78
Skewness of 94 observations	=	0.78
RESULTS OF TURNING POINT TEST		
Reduce variate Z	=	0.41
Interpretation : SERIES IS RANDOM		
RESULT OF KENDALL'S CO-RELATION TEST		
Reduce variate z	=	1.42
Interpretation : NO TREND EXISTS		
SLOPE SIGNIFICANT TEST		
Test statistic	=	1.59
Degree of Freedom	=	92
STOCHASTIC ANALYSIS		
PERSON-III TRANSFORMATION		
Mean of the (transformed) series	=	-0.003
Standeed deviation of the (transformed) series	=	1.023
Skewness of the (transformed) series	=	-0.235
Chi-square test statistics	=	8.894
Degree of freedom	=	3

ii) Water quality

Information pertaining to the quality of the ground water resources - which form the sole basis of water supply to the town of Roorkee - is available only from 1980.

Ionic balance checks (Sawyer, 1985) were conducted to ascertain the correctness of the available water quality data (Table 5.13). The checks indicate that results are acceptable.

The ionic concentrations of 1980 and 1989 were plotted on the pattern of Piper's trilinear diagram (Figure 5.17). The results indicate that there was a significant increase in hardness of water in 1989 compared to 1980.

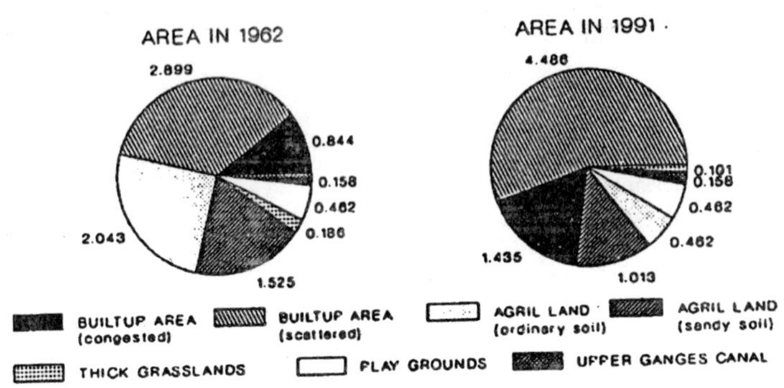

Fig. 5.15 : Landuse pattern in Roorkee

iii) Expected pollution of ground water by waste disposal practices

As the sole source of water supply to the town of Roorkee is from underground, the present waste disposal pattern was studied to see whether any possibility exits of it affecting the ground water.

Figure 5.18 shows the post-monsoon and pre-monsoon water-table contours for the years 1977 and 1989. Dotted lines and firm lines show the contours corresponding to pre-monsoon and post-monsoon water levels respectively. It is clear that the pattern of groundwater flow has not changed over the years. Further, the areas shown in the figure belong to a single contiguous aquifer. As such the present disposal site for the roughly 200 tones per day garbage as also the town's sewage, is situated upstream of the aquifer. There is thus vary strong possibility of the present waste disposal site causing contamination of the entire aquifer supporting the present water supply. This impact is expected to be most severe during post monsoon when the water-table as well as the infiltration rates are high, facilitating contamination.

Table 5.10 :
Runoff calculation using SCS method

OVERVIEW OF SCS METHOD

A first step in the use of the SCS model is to estimate the volume of direct runoff, by expression

$$Q = \frac{(P\text{-}Ia)^2}{(P\text{-}Ia)+S} * \text{Area} \qquad \text{... (1)}$$

where,

P = the volume of rainfall
Ia = the initial abstraction, and
S = A retention parameter

Conceptually Ia represents the interception, infiltration and surface storage process that occur before runoff begins, SCS allowed the following approximation for the initial abstraction.

$$Ia = 0.20S \qquad \text{... (2)}$$

Substituting Ia in equation (I)

$$Q = \frac{(P\text{-}0.20S)^2}{P+0.8S} * \text{Area} \qquad \text{... (3)}$$

$$Q = 0 \text{ if } P \leq 0.20S$$

The potential maximum retention S (inch) related to a curve number (CN) by the empirical expression

$$CN = \frac{1000}{S+10}$$

$$S(\text{inch}) = \frac{1000}{CN} - 10 \quad \text{or} \quad S(\text{cm}) = \frac{2540}{CN} - 25.4 \qquad \text{....4}$$

and curve number

$$CN = \frac{\sum \text{Area of the different soils} * CN}{\text{Total Area}} \qquad \text{(Saeed, 1987)}$$

The above described methodology is adopted for estimating runoff as illustrated on the next pages.

TAble 5.10 *Cont....*

1967

Category	Area %	Area Sq.Km	CN Value	Area * CN value	
Built up Area(Cong)	10.4	0.844	90	75.96	
Built up Area(Scatt)	35.7	2.899	85	246.415	Total CN
Agricultural Land(Ord)	25.2	2.043	71	145.053	=
Agricultural Land(Snd)	18.8	1.525	78	118.95	635.05
Thick Grassland		2.3	0.186	58	10.788
/Area					
Playgrounds	5.7	0.462	82	37.884	79.80220

$S_{(1967)} = 2540/79.81 - 25.4 = 6.43.$

1990

Category	Area %	Area Sq.Km	CN Value	Area * CN value	
Built up Area(Cong)	17.7	1.435	90	129.15	
Built up Area(Scatt)	55.3	4.486	85	381.31	Total CN
Agricultural Land(Ord)	5.7	0.462	71	32.802	=
Agricultural Land(Snd)	12.5	1.013	78	79.014	666.018
Thick Grassland	1.3	0.101	58	5.858	/Area
Playgrounds	5.7	0.462	82	37.884	83.70214

$S_{(1990)} = 2540/83.70 - 25.4 = 4.95$

1967			1990		
Rainfall (cm)	Runoff (cm)	Runoff (cub.m)	Rainfall (cm)	Runoff (cm)	Runoff (cub.m)
10	5.016098	399231.2	10	5.817559	463019.5

$$\% \text{ Change in Runoff} = \frac{399231.2 - 463019}{399231.2} = 15.97\ \%$$

TABLE 5.11 :
Withdrawl (postmonsoon level- Premonsoon level (next year) and recharge (postmonsoon level - premonsoon level) data, 1973-1994

Year	Pre Monsoon	Post Monsoon	Withdrawl	Recharge
1973	260.88	263.36	2.48	
1974	261	262.47	2.36	1.47
1975	259.78	262.18	2.69	2.4
1976	259.22	263.2	2.96	3.98
1977	259.67	261.9	3.53	2.23
1978	260.14	262.8	1.76	2.66
1979	258.85	261.1	3.95	2.25
1980	259.5	261.98	1.6	2.48
1981	259.84	261.17	2.14	1.33
1982	259.97	261.36	1.2	1.39
1983	259.73	261.74	1.63	2.01
1984	260.61	263.55	1.13	2.94
1985	260.61	263.54	2.94	2.93
1986	261.41	262.13	2.13	0.72
1987	259.59	259.95	2.54	0.36
1988	258.93	262.93	1.02	4
1989	259.89	263.16	3.04	3.27
1990	258.14	262.24	5.02	4.1
1991	259.74	263.23	2.5	3.49
1992	260.1	262.2	3.13	2.1
1993	258.93	263.85	3.27	4.92
1994	261	263.13	2.85	2.13

TABLE 5.12 :
Trend analysis of groundwater withdrawl in Roorkee

SMART ALEC

(c) Pondicherry University
TREND ANALYSIS AND FORECASTING
Parameter : WATER-WITHDRAWL
TREND ANALYSIS

Number of observations	=	21
Mean of 21 observations	=	2.54
Standard deviation of 21 observations	=	0.99
Skewness of 21 observations	=	0.51

RESULTS OF TURNING POINT TEST

Reduce variate Z	=	1.26

Interpretation : SERIES IS NOT RANDOM
RESULT OF KENDALL'S CO-RELATION TEST

(Cont.....)

Reduce variate z	=	0.72
Interpretation : NO TREND EXISTS		
SLOPE SIGNIFICANT TEST		
Test statistic	=	0.77
Degree of Freedom	=	19
STOCHASTIC ANALYSIS		
CHOW'S LOGNORMAL TRANSFORMATION		
Mean of the (transformed) series	=	0.863
Standeed deviation of the (transformed) series	=	0.375
Skewness of the (transformed) series	=	-0.499
Chi-square test statistics	=	4.429
Degree of freedom	=	3

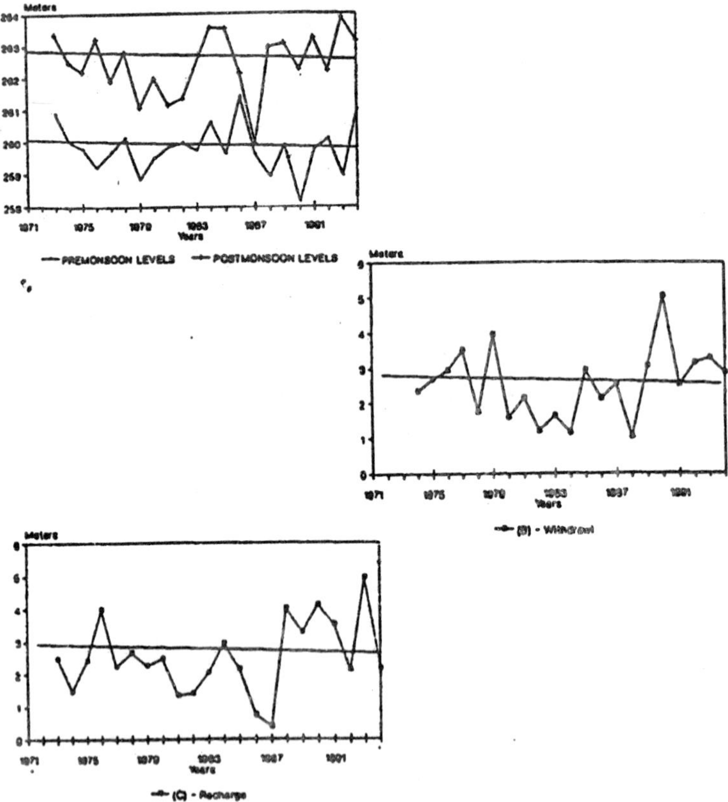

Fig. 5.16 : a) ground table,
b) impact of withdrawl on the GW table, and
c) impact of recharge on GW

TABLE 5.13 :
Ionic balance check for water quality

Ion	At.Wt	Eq.wt	Constituent		EPM			
			1980	1989	Fe 1980	AI	Fe 1986	AI
SO_4^-	96	48	119	13	2.48	2.48	0.27	0.27
Cl^-35.5	35.5	57	7	1.61	1.61	0.20	0.20	
HCO_3^-	61	61	239	273	3.92	3.92	4.48	4.48
Total					8.01	8.01	4.95	4.95
Si^{+++}	28	9.33	17	5	1.82	1.82	0.54	0.54
Fe^{+++}	56	18.7	31	3	1.66		0.16	
Al^{+++}	27	9				3.44		0.33
Ca^{++}	40	20	10	32	0.5	0.5	0.54	0.54
Mg^{++}	24	12	31	14	2.58	2.58	2.58	2.58
Na^+	23	23	19	31	0.83	0.83	0.83	0.83
Total					7.39	9.17	4.82	4.99

FIRST CHECK

Ionic balance is O.K., if $A \leq B$

where ,

$$A = | \Sigma \text{ Anion} - \Sigma \text{ Cation} |$$

& $$B = 0.1065 + 0.0155 \Sigma \text{ Anion}$$

So, $A_{80(Fe)}$ $= | 8.01 - 7.39 | = 0.62$

$A_{80(Al)}$ $= | 8.01 - 9.17 || = 1.16$

$A_{89(Fe}$ $= |4.95 - 4.82 | = 0.13$

$A_{89(Al}$ $= |4.95 - 4.99| = 0.014$

B_{89} $= 0.1065 + 0.0155 * 4.95 = 0.1832$

B_{80} $= 0.1065 + 0.0155 * 8.01 = 0.231$

In all the cases $A \leq B$ therefore, ionic balance is O.K. except $A_{80(Fe)} \geq B_{80}$ that means ionic balance for Fe in 1980 is not correctly analysed.

SECOND CHECK

Ratio of TDS to EC should be between 0.6 to 0.9

Ratio in 1980 = 446/719 = 0.62 ,and

Ratio in 1989 = 322/480 = 0.67

So,both the cases TDS/EC ratio is acceptable.

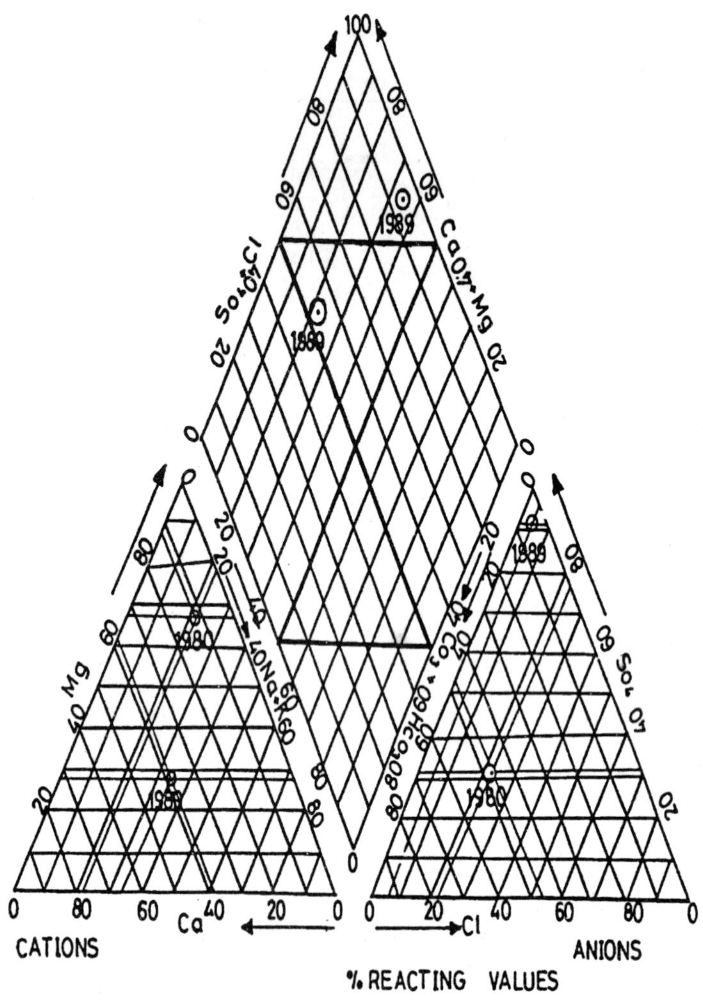

Fig. 5.17 : Piper's trilinear diagram for representative water samples.

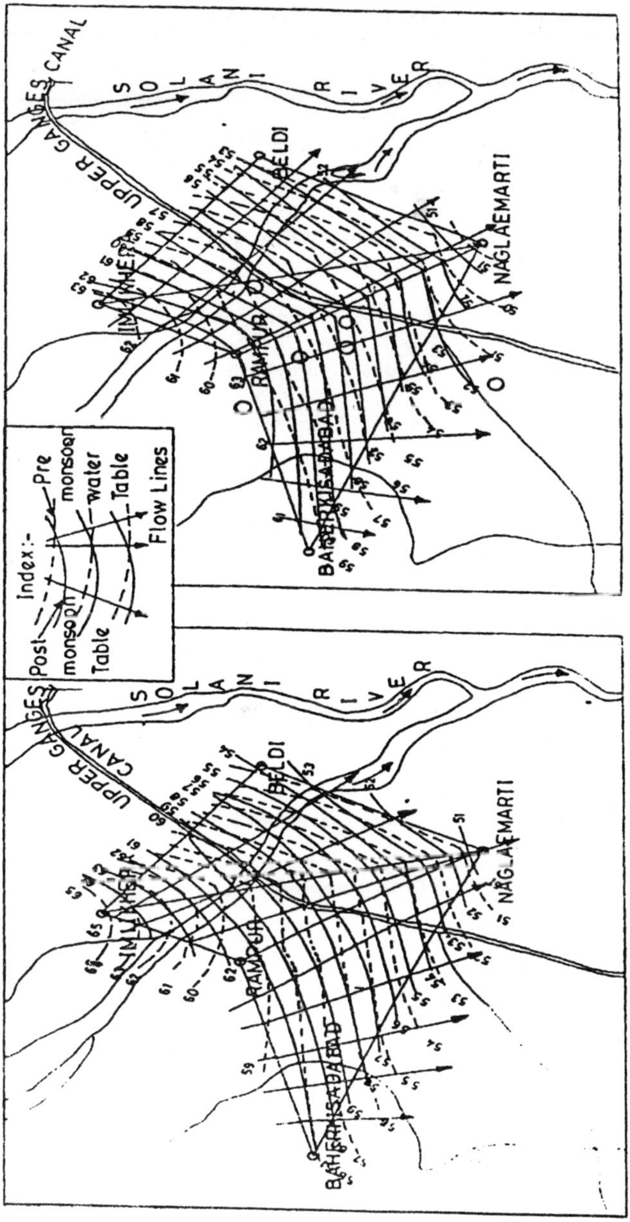

Fig. 5.18 : Pattern of ground water flow in Roorkee.

ANNEXURE
(SUMMARY OF THE TESTS USED IN SMART-ALEC)

Name of the test and the source	Key Equations
	SUBROUTINE BASICSTAT
Arithmetic Mean (Levin, 1990)	Arithmetic mean, $\overline{X} = \frac{\sum_{i=1}^{N} X_i}{N}$
Median (Levin, 1990)	If number of observation are odd, the medium is (N+1)/2th item of the series otherwise the median is arithmetic mean of (N/2)th and (N+1)/2th term.
Mode (Kapoor, 1991)	Mode = 3 * Median - 2 * Mean
Root Mean Square Value (Spiegel, 1981)	$R.M.S = \sqrt{(\sum_{i=i}^{N} X^2) / N}$
Range (Levin, 1990)	Range = (Maximum - Minimum) value
Standard Deviation (Kapoor, 1991)	Standard Deviation, $S = \sqrt{\frac{1}{N}\sum_{i=1}^{N} x-\overline{x})^2}$
Variance (Kapoor, 1991)	Variance = (Standard Deviation)^2
Skewness (Kapoor, 1991)	

SUBROUTINE RANDOMNESS CHECK

Turning Point Test
(Kumar, 1983; NIH, 1988)
(Kumar, 1983; NIH, 1988)

Turning point (Tp) are
$Y_{i-1} < Y_i > Y_{i+1}$ or
$Y_{i-1} > Y_i < Y_{i+1}$
Expected value of turning points
E(Tp) = 2(N-2)/3
Variance of V(Tp) = (16N - 29) / 90
Tp-E(Tp)

$$\text{Reduce variate } Z = \frac{Tp - E(Tp)}{\sqrt{V(Tp)}}$$

If Z is between ± 1.96 then the series is random.

SUBROUTINE TREND ANALYSIS

Kendall's Test
(NIH, 1988)

The test statistics, Z =

$$\text{where, } = \frac{4P}{N(N-1)} - 1$$

(P is total number of observations exceeding the previous value); and

$$\text{Var}(\tau) = \frac{2(2N+5)}{9N(N-1)}$$

If êZ ê > 1.96	⇒	trend exists;
if Z is < -1.96	⇒	falling trend; and
if Z is > +1.96	⇒	rising trend.

Regression Test
(NIH, 1988)

Equation of a straight line is
Y = a+b X
t- statistics of gradient, $t = B/SE_b$
where,

$$\text{gradient, } b = d^2 = \frac{\sum_{i=i}^{N} (Yi+1-Yi)^2}{(N-1)}$$

and standard error of gradient,

$$SE_b = \left[\frac{\sum_{i=1}^{N} (Yi - \overline{X})^2 - b^2 \sum_{i=1}^{N} (Xi - \overline{X})^2}{(N-2) \sum_{i=1}^{N} (Xi - \overline{X})} \right]$$

If, $t_{calculated} < t_{(1-0.5a\ ,\ (N-2))}$
then trend is statistically approved.
Where, a is significance level, and
(N-2) is degree of freedom.

Mean Square Sucessive Difference Test (Wa;;. 1986)

Test statistics, $Z = \dfrac{(d2/2)/S^2 - 1}{\sqrt{(N-2)(N-1)}}$

where,

$$S^2 = \left[\frac{\sum_{i=i}^{N} Yi^2 \left(\sum_{i=i}^{N} Yi^2\right)/N}{(N-1)} \right]$$

and

$$d^2 = \frac{\sum_{i=i}^{N} (Yi + 1 - Yi)^2}{(N-1)}$$

Negative value of Z would mean long-term trend or slow-oscillations; +ve would mean *vice-versa*.

SUBROUTINE STOCHASTIC ANALYSIS

Normal Distribution (Seth, 1985)
The data is checked for the normal distribution

Inverse Pearson Type III Transformation (Seth, 1985)

Y' =

$$Y' = \left[\left(\frac{Ca}{2}\left(\frac{Y-\bar{Y}}{S}\right)\right)+1\right]\frac{6}{C3}+\frac{Cs}{6}$$

Log Normal Transformation (Seth, 1985)

$$\mu = \log_e(\bar{Y}) - 0.5 \log_e \left[\left[\frac{S}{Y}\right]^2 + 1\right]$$

$$= \left[\log_e\left[\frac{S}{Y}\right]^2 + 1\right]^{1/2}$$

Log Transformation (Seth, 1985)

$Y' = \log_e X$

Inverse Log Pearson Type III Transformationlog (Seth, 1985)
In Inverse Log Pearson Type III distribution transformed series is used instead of the original series.

Square Root Transormation (Seth, 1985)

$Y' = (X)^{1/2}$

SUBROUTINE HYPOTHESIS TESTING

t-Statistics (Doane, 1985)
Standard error of two means from the same population

$$SE_{x-y} = \sqrt{\frac{(N_x-1)\,S^2_y+(N_y-1)S^2_y}{N_x+N_y-2}}$$

$$* \sqrt{\frac{1}{N_x}+\frac{1}{N_y}}$$

Test Statistics, $t = \dfrac{\bar{X} - \bar{Y}}{SE_{\bar{x}-\bar{y}}}$

Chi-square Test

(Davis, 1973; Seth, 1985)

$$\sum_{i=1}^{k} \frac{(O_i - E_i)^2}{E_i}$$

Lilifor's Test

a) Standize the data by $Z = \dfrac{Y - \bar{Y}}{S}$

b) Find out normal probability (Np) of corresponding Zp.

c) Find out sample probability by Sp=I/N
I : datum level (1,2,......., N)

d) Calculate the difference

$d_a = [Np_{(i)} - Sp_{(i)}]$ and

$d_b = [Np(i+1) - Sp(i)]$

The test statistic will be the largest value of d_a or d_b

SUBROUTINE CO-RELATION ANALYSIS

Simple Co-relation Coefficient

(Makridakis, 1987)

Co-relation coefficient between X and Y,

$$r_{xy} = \frac{Cov_{xy}}{\sqrt{Cov_{xy} * Cov_{yy}}}$$

where,

$$Cov_{xy} = \frac{1}{N} \sum_{i=1}^{N} (X_i - \bar{X}) * (Y_i - \bar{Y})$$

SUBROUTINE ANOVA

One way ANOVA

(Davis, 1973)

Sum of squares between rows,

$$SSA = \sum_{k=1}^{k} \frac{T^2_k}{N_k} - \frac{T^2}{N}$$

Total sum of squares,

$$SST = \sum_{j=1}^{J} \sum_{k=1}^{K} X2 - \frac{T^2}{N}$$

Sampling error, SSE = SST - SSA

Mean square value between rows,

$$MSA = \frac{SSA}{K\text{-}1}$$

Mean square of error, $MSE = \frac{SSE}{N\text{-}K}$

$$F_{(K\text{-}1)(N\text{-}K)} = \frac{MSA}{MSE}$$

Two way ANOVA

Sum of squares between rows,

$$SSA = \sum_{K=1}^{K} \frac{T_k^2}{N_k} - \frac{T^2}{N}$$

Sum of squares between columns,

$$SSB = \frac{1}{K} \sum_{I=1}^{J} T^2_j - \frac{T^2}{N}$$

Total sum of squres,

$$SST = \sum_{J=1}^{J}$$

Sampling error, SSE = SST-SSA-SSB

Mean square value between rows,

$$MSA = \frac{SSA}{K\text{-}1}$$

Mean square value between columns,

$$MSA = \frac{SSA}{J\text{-}1}$$

Mean square of error, MSE $= \dfrac{SSE}{(j-1)\ (K-1)}$

$$FI_{(K-1)(N-K)} = \frac{MSA}{MSE}$$

$$F2(j-1)(N-K) = \frac{MSB}{MSE}$$

If the calculated F is greater than the tabulated F for the specified level of significance - then the hypothsis of several sample means came from the same population, is rejected.

SUBROUTINE REGRESSION ANALYSIS

Linear Regression (Davis, 1973)

$$Y_i = b_o + b_i X_i$$

$$\sum_{i=1}^{N} (Y_i - y_i)^2 \text{ should be minimized}$$

$$\sum_{i=1}^{N} Y_i = b_o n + b_1 \sum_{i=1}^{N} Xi$$

$$\sum_{i=1}^{N} X_i Y_i = b_o \sum_{i=1}^{N} X_i + bi \sum_{i=1}^{N} Xi^2$$

These equations can be solved by the method of matrices for b_o and b_1

$$\begin{bmatrix} N & \sum X \\ \sum X & \sum X^2 \end{bmatrix} \begin{bmatrix} b_0 \\ b_1 \end{bmatrix} = \begin{bmatrix} \sum Y \\ \sum XY \end{bmatrix}$$

Linear Transformation (Davis, 1973)

Following equations can be fitted as linear regression equation:

<u>(i) Exponential transformation</u>

$$Y_i = b_o . e^{b1xi}$$

taking log of both sides

$\log_e (Yi) = \log_e (b_o) + b_1 X_i$

(ii) Power transformation

$Y_i = b_o . X_i^{b1}$

taking log of both sides

$\log_e Y_i = \log_e b_o + b_1 \log_e X_i$

(iii) Saturation transformation

$$Y_i = b_o \frac{Xi}{Xi+b1} \text{ or}$$

$$\frac{1}{Y_i} = \frac{1}{b_o} + \frac{b_1}{b_o} \left[\frac{1}{X_i} \right]$$

Polynomial Regression

$$Y_i = b_o + b_1 X_i + b_2 X_i^2 + b_3 X_i^3 + \ldots\ldots\ldots b_m X_i^m$$

The method described earlier holds except for the fact that the number of variables have increased.

A least square solution to a linear equations of this type can be found by solving a set of normal equations for the b coefficients. These can be expressed in matrix form as

$$[\Sigma[X]\ [b]=\Sigma Y]$$

and solution is

$$[b]=[x]^{-1}[\Sigma Y]$$

SUBROUTINE FORECASTING ANALYSIS

Single Moving Average
(Jarrett, 1987)

$$\frac{X_t + X_{t-1} + \ldots + X_{t-N+1}}{N}$$

Double Moving Average
(Jarrett, 1987)

$$\frac{1}{N}\left[\sum_{i=t-N+1}^{N} X_i\right]$$

$$S_t = \left[\sum_{i=t-N+1}^{N} X_i\right]$$

$$S_t' = \sum_{i=t}^{t-N+1} S_i / N$$

Equation for forecast is

$F_{t+m} = a_t + b_t m.$

where, $a_t = 2S_t - S''_t$
and bt =

Single Exponential Smoothing
(Jarrett, 1987)

Basic model, $F_{t+1} = \alpha X_t + (1-\alpha) F_t$

Double Exponential Smoothing
(Jarrett, 1987)

$S_t = \alpha X_t + (1-\alpha) S_{t-1}$

$S''_t = \alpha S_t + (1-\alpha) S''_{t-1}$

The Equation for forecast is

$F_{t+m} = a_t + b_t m.$
where, $a_t = 2S_t - S''_t$

and $b_t = \frac{2}{n-1}(S''_t - S_t)$

Quadratic Exponential Smoothing
(Jarrett, 1987)

$S_t = \alpha X_t + (1-\alpha) S_{t-1}$

$S''_t = \alpha S_t + (1-\alpha) S''_{t-1}$

$S''_t = \alpha S'_t + (1 - \alpha) S''t - 1$

Equation for forecast is

$F_{t+m} = a_t + b_t m + 0.5 c_t m^2$

where

$a_t = 3 S_t - 3 S_t' + S_t''$

$$bt = \frac{\alpha}{2(1 - \alpha)^2} *$$

$$[(6-5\alpha) S_t - (10 - 8\alpha) S_t' + (4 - 3\alpha) S_t'']$$

and

$$c_t = \frac{\alpha}{(1 - \alpha)^2} (S_t - 2 S_t' + S''_t)$$

ABBREVIATIONS / SYMBOLS USED

X_i	:	X data series
X	:	Mean of X data
Y_i	:	Y data series
Y	:	Mean of Y data
N	:	Total number of observations
S	:	Standard deviation
Tp	:	Number of turning points
E(TP)	:	Expected value of turning points
V(Tp)	:	Variance of turning points
Z	:	Reduced variate
P	:	Total number of observations exceeding the previous one
B	:	Gradient or slope of a line
SE	:	Standard error
Y'	:	Transformed series
m	:	Mean of transformed series
s	:	Standard deviation of transformed series
C_s	:	Coefficient of skewness
k	:	Number of classes in chi-square test
O_i	:	Observed number of data points in a class
E_i	:	Expected number of data points in a class
N_p	:	Standard normal probability
S_p	:	Sample probability
I	:	datum level
T_i	:	Row wise sum
T^2	:	Sum of the squares of T_i.
K	:	Number of rows
J	:	Number of columns
r	:	Coefficient of co-relation
cov	:	Co-variance
y_i	:	Estimated values of Y series by least square method
$b_{0,1,..}$	:	constants of a equation
St'	:	Predicted values by single moving average or single exponentials smoothing methods
St"	:	Predicted values by double moving average or double exponential smoothing methods
S_t'''	:	Predicted values by triple exponential smoothing method
a	:	Smoothing constant
m	:	Order of the polynomial

6

CREAM - A NEW APPROACH FOR ASSESSING `TOTAL IMPACTS' AND DETERMINING STRATEGIES FOR ENVIRONMENTALLY SUSTAINABLE DEVELOPMENTAL PLANNING

INTRODUCTION

An EIA is considered complete only after all the relevant variables, at least all the ones that have significant impacts, have been assessed, individually as well as collectively, to get a holistic perspective of the system under study. In the earlier chapters we have described studies on the nexus between the various variables of the system and the impact on it, of individual variables, and vice-versa. In this chapter we present a methodology that we have developed to understand the system *as a whole*. The methodology is based on network analysis. A software CREAM (Computer-aided Rapid Environmental impact Assessment and Management) has been developed on the basis of this methodology. Typical print outs of cream are shown in Figure 6.1(a-i). The methodology has been applied to generate and evaluate developmental scenarios for the city of Roorkee.

6.2 METHODOLOGICAL DETAILS OF CREAM

6.2.1 Problem structure

i) Problem tree

a) Environment consists of myriad interconnected and interdependent aspects. Each of these can be characterized by some basic indicator. To analyse the whole system, basic indicators of each aspects of the environment need be studied and out of these the most relevant ones are to be selected to represent the system as holistically as practicable. We have called these indicators as *basic indicators* or *first-level variables.*

b) These indicators may be grouped under broad categories based on the particular aspect of the environment they indicate: economic, sociocultural, etc. (Table 6.1). We have termed categories as *second-level variables.*

c) The second-level variables may be further grouped to form the *third-level variables,* and so on. (Table 6.1)

d) Second -level variables, or further levels if any, are collectively termed as *composite indicators.*

ii) Ideal and worst value of variables

Each basic indicator is to be assigned an *ideal* value and a *worst* value. These may be assigned on the basis of any of these criteria:

a) values that are indicated as 'ideal' by environmental standards (for example zero BOD is an ideal value for a river water according to water quality standards);

b) values that we know as ideal or more precisely 'best achievable' from past experience or knowledge (for example yield of fish from a river or harvest of rice from a farm; the best achieved in the past may be set as 'ideal'); and

c) values we may want to be attained (example a population growth rate of zero or eradication of a disease).

iii) Weighing the variables

Each basic indicator is to be assigned a value which would show the extent of importance of the indicator. The weightage is to be

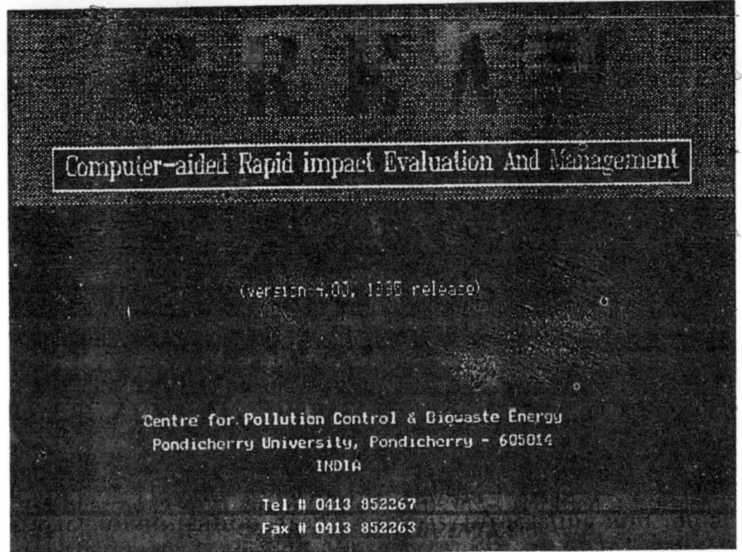

Figure 6.1a: Software package CREAM

assigned in such a way that the sum of all values in one group should total one. In order to determine these weightages either a Delphi may be conducted or use of standards can be made. The same method applies to second, third, *et al.* levels of variables (Table 6.2).

6.2.2 Analysis

The next stage is to analyse the data. This would consist of the following steps.

i) Since units of most the of indicator variables are different from each other (such as of population density and water level) a trade-off analysis is done in order to normalize the values; in other words transformation of all the units is done so as to have them fall between 0 and 1. To do this normalization either of the following general equations are used.

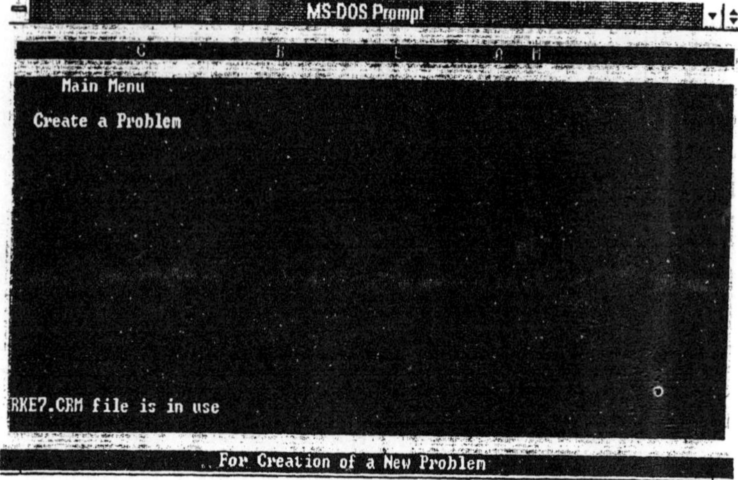

Figure 6.1b: Main menu of CREAM

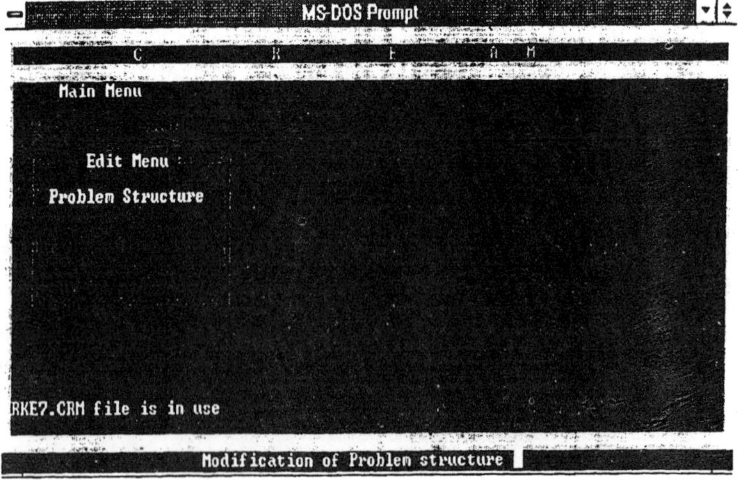

Figure 6.1e: Edit menu of the software

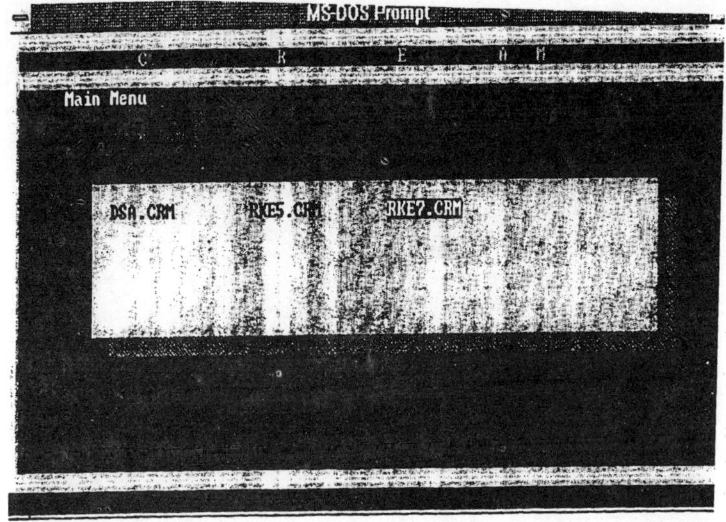

Figure 6.1d: File reading in CREAM

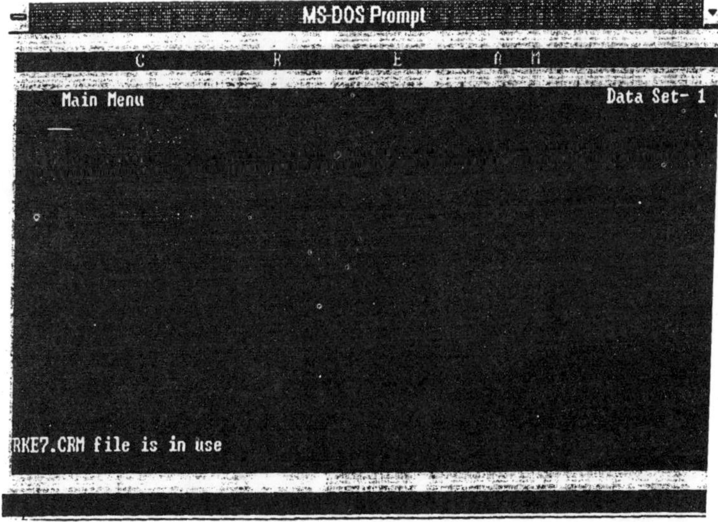

Figure 6.1e: A typical data entry

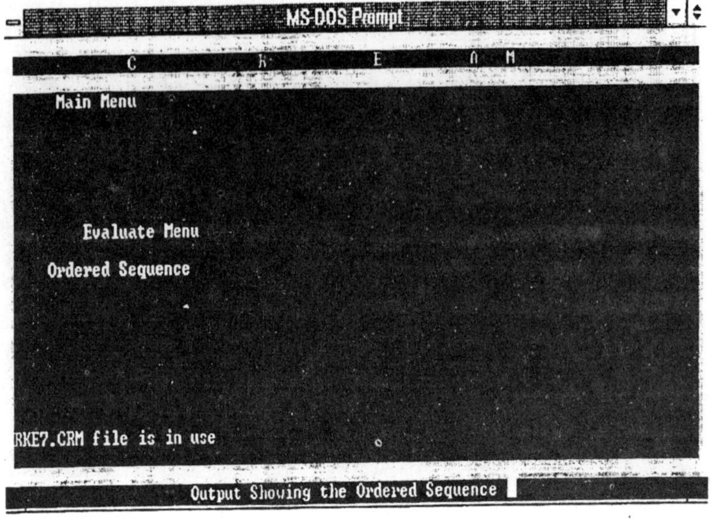

Figure 6.1f: Options available for evaluating a problem

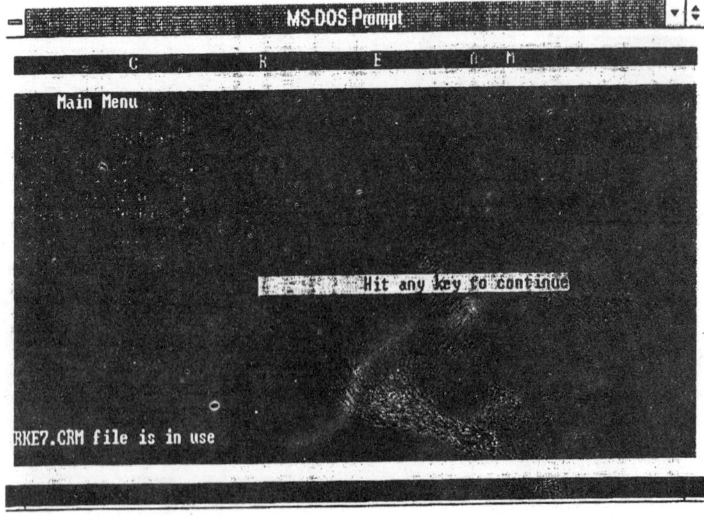

Figure 6.1g: A typical output of final scores of the system.

MS-DOS Prompt

C R E A M

Problem Structure & Importance

	LEVEL 1	IMPORTANCE
	▸Temperature(max)	0.50
▸Climate	▸Temperature(min)	0.50
▸Terrestrial	▸Landuse	1.00
▸Aquatic	▸Water levels	1.00
	▸Population density	0.25
	▸Birth death ratio	0.20
	▸Literacy ratio	0.20
	▸Health ratio	0.25
▸Social	▸Power availability	0.10
	▸Occupational Str	0.40
	▸Financial reciepts	0.22
	▸Transportation	0.12
▸Economy	▸Expenditure	0.26

LEVEL 2 IMPORTANCE

Figure 6.1h: Report of detailed analysis

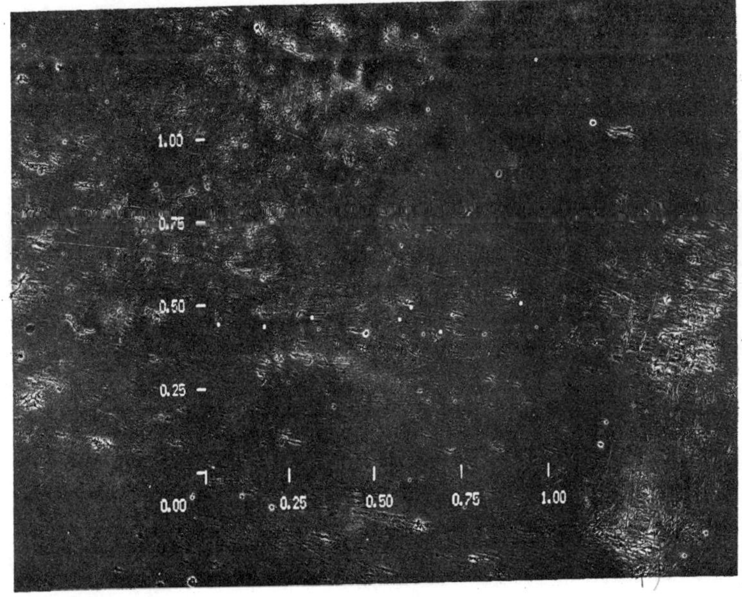

Figure 6.1i: Graphical representation of the results.

$$\text{Normalised value} = \left| \frac{\text{Worst value - Actual value}}{\text{Ideal values - Worst value}} \right| \quad \ldots 6.1$$

or

$$\text{Normalised value} = \left\{ 1 - \left| \frac{\text{Ideal value - Actual value}}{\text{Ideal values - Worst value}} \right| \right\} \quad \ldots 6.2$$

For example : water level fluctuation is 3.04 meter in the year 1991 (Table 6.5); its *ideal* and *worst* values are 0.25 meter and 3.42 meter (Table 6.4). If we use equation 6.1 the normalized value is $|(3.42-3.04)/(0.25-3.42)| = 0.120$; the same value is obtained if we use equation 6.2 $(1-|(0.25-3.04)/(0.25-3.42)|) = 0.12$.

ii) The normalized values indicate the departure or distance (L_1) of the indicator from its ideal state, 1.

iii) Once distances of each basic indicator from its ideal value are determined, the distances (L_2) of the second level variables can be determined by the function:

$$L_{i,j} = \sum (\alpha_{j.k} \cdot L_{i-1,j}) \quad \ldots 6.3$$

where, a = weighting values

i = level number

j = indicator number in a group

k = group number

iv) Similarly, third-level distances and that of further levels, if any are deter mined. This process is continued till it gives a single value. This particular value is the composite representation of the system as shown in Table 6.3.

6.2.3 Graphical representation of the results

In order to get the gist of the abovementioned analysis in easily comprehendable form, the results are represented graphically - a typical output is given in Figure 6.2. The essential features of the graphical output are :

i) both x-axis and y-axis have the scale from 0-1, where 0 represents the worst value and 1 the ideal value;

ii) the *zone of unacceptability, zone of compromise,* and the ideal zone are represented as clearly marked segments. The lines demarkating these segments are drawn by giving appropriate L values (in case of Figure 4.2 they are ≤ 0.4 for *unacceptable zone,* < 0.4 < 0.7 for *zone of compromise* and ≥ for the *ideal zone*) to equation 6.3 and calculating the coordinate of demarkation lines.

6.3 APPLICATION OF THE CREAM TO ROORKEE

6.3.1 Definition of base level indicators

The indicator structure used in this application are described in Chapter-III.

6.3.2 Weighing factors

The weighing factors (a) assigned in the analysis, are presented in Table 6.2. The factors were subjectively chosen in the present case, based on intuitive judgment, but these can also be obtained using standard Delphi procedures (Benarie, 1988).

6.3.3 Ideal and worst values

Ideal and worst values for each indicator are tabulated in Table 6.4 . These have been set as follows. For parameters 1,2,4,5,10,12 and 13 the most and the least acceptable values have been taken from the last 94 years'(1901-1994) data. For example the least of the yearly maximum temperatures recorded during the 1901-1991 span (41 c) has been set as the realistic *ideal* maximum temperature and the highest recorded temperature in the span (46.7 c) has been set as the *worst.* For parameter 3 the lowest recorded builtup area : total area ratio has been set as the *ideal* while the maximum possible value for the ratio (1) has been set as the *worst.*

For parameters 6,7 and 9 the best attainable state has been set as *ideal* while the worst recorded state has been taken as *worst.* For parameter 11 the worst possible situation of zero receipts has been set as the *worst* frame of reference ; the best values attained so far has been set as the *ideal.*

TABLE 6.1 :
Indicator structure of CREAM for EIA of the development of Roorkee

	Composite indicators	Basic indicators		System
		second-level	third-level	
1.	Temperature (max)			
2.	Temperature (min)	Climate		
3.	Land use	Terrestrial	Environ	
4.	Water levels	Aquatic	-ment	
5.	Population density			
6.	Birth death ratio			System
7.	Literacy ratio	Social		
8.	Health ratio			
9.	Power availability		Socio-	
10	Occupational structure		economy	
11	Financial receipts			
12	Transportation (roads)			
13	Expenditure			

TABLE 6.2:
Weighing factors (α)

	Basic indicators		Composite Indicators			
		α	second-level	α	third-level	α
1.	Temperature (max)	0.50				
2.	Temperature (min)	0.50	Climate	0.26		
3.	Land use	1.00	Terrestrial	0.37	Environment	0.5
4.	Water levels	1.00	Aquatic	0.37		
5.	Population density	0.25				
6.	Birth death ratio	0.20				
7.	Literacy ratio	0.20	Social	0.60		
8.	Health ratio	0.25				
9.	Power availability	0.10				
	Socio-					
10	Occupational structure	0.40				
	economy	0.5				
11	Financial receipts	0.22	Economy	0.40		
12	Transportation (roads)	0.12				
13	Expenditure	0.26				

TABLE 6.3 :
Pattern of analysis at different levels considered in CREAM

$L_{1,j} = 1 - \dfrac{W_i - A_i}{I_i - W_i}$		$L_{2,j} = \Sigma L_1 \cdot IV_1$	$L_{3,j} = L_2 \cdot IV_2$	$L_{4,j} = \Sigma L_3 \cdot IV_3$	
1. Temperature(max)	0.000				
2. Temperature(min)	0.462	Climate	0.231		
3. Land use	0.519	Terrestrial	0.519	Environment	0.296
4. Water levels	0.120	Aquatic	0.120		
5. Population density	0.951				
6. Birth death ratio	0.196				
7. Literacy ratio	0.302	Social	0.502		0.405
8. Health ratio	0.304				
9. Power availability	0.781				
			Socio-		
10 Occupational structure	0.625				
economy	0.514				
11 Financial receipts	0.742		Economy		0.534
12 Transportation(roads)	0.417				
13 Expenditure	0.271				

Where,

W : Worst Value
I : Ideal Value
A : Actual Value
IV_i : Importance Values at level 1,2,3,....etc.
L : Distances at levels 1,2,3,....etc.

6.3.4 Analysis of the system states

The values of these indicators were calculated from the data for Roorkee for the period 1961-1994 (Table 6.5). The data was collected from myriad sources and is given in Chapter-III. The indicator values for the years 2001, 2011 and 2021 were obtained by extrapolating the 1961-1994 data using regression analysis, performed with software package SMART-ALEC (Chapter-V) assuming that the past trends would be persisting in future.

The results are summarised in Figure 6.2. The analysis reveals that the pattern of development till 1961 was environmentally compatible. In subsequent years the stress due to development

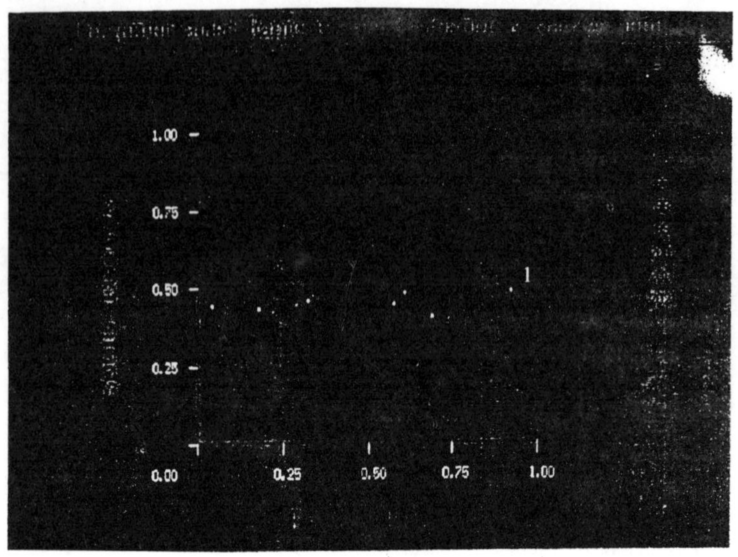

Figure 6.2: Possitions of system state (of the city of Roorkee) if the existing trends persist.

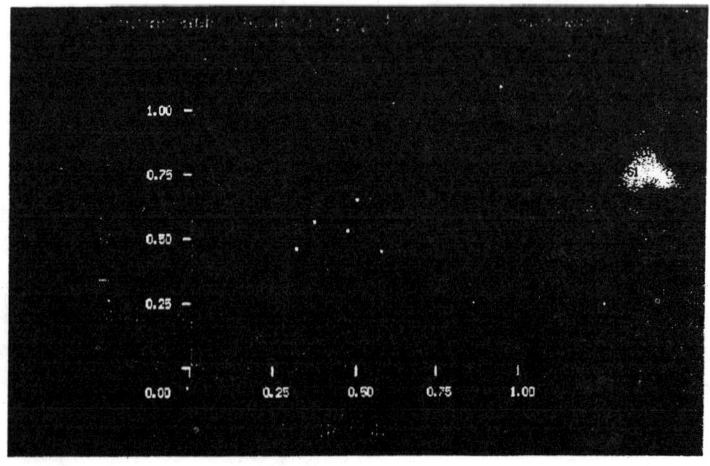

Figure 6.3: The system states achievable in 2001 AD with development scenarios G1, G2 and G3.

began to unsettle the environment and the system state is passing through a *zone of compromise* from the 1960s. In each passing decade the system state is drifting farther and farther away from environmentally compatible zone and by 2001 it would cross the threshold of *zone of compromise* and will enter the zone of unacceptability.

Figure 6.2 presents graphically how close or far the past system states, and the forecasts, are from the *ideal* state.

6.3.5 Sensitivity analysis

Sensitivity analysis was performed employing the data from Tables 6.5 and 6.6 by varying the weighing factors (Table 6.2). The findings in brief are:

i) at the level III, the system state was more sensitive to environmental/ecological than socio-economic factors;
ii) at the level II the system state was most sensitive to terrestrial and aquatic indicators; and
iii) at the base level, the indicators governing the system state most strongly were land-use pattern and water level.

TABLE 6.4 :
Ideal and *worst* values

Indicators	Values	
	Ideal	Worst
1. Temperature(max)	41.00	46.70
2. Temperature(min)	3.60	1.00
3. Land use	0.46	1.00
4. Water levels	0.25	3.42
5. Population density	4480	14572
6. Birth death ratio	1.00	5.53
7. Literacy ratio	1.00	0.57
8. Health ratio	2.00	0.11
9. Power availability	1.00	0.27
10. Occupational structure	0.28	0.20
11. Financial receipts	28.76	0.00
12. Transportation(roads)	267.90	55.00
13. Expenditure	9.80	123.00

6.3.6 Analysis of the development policies

These findings were conveyed to the Municipal Council of the city of Roorkee. They considered these findings in the context of their developmental priorities and availability of resources and zeroed on three sets of desirable goals, or scenarios, presented as G1, G2 and G3 in Table 6.7. These scenarios were worked out by them towards realisation of the following alternatives.

i) Development option G1

1. Increasing the Municipal area by 8 km with a mandatory 20% open area.
2. Introducing intermittent Water supply (reduction by 7 hrs/ day) i.e 200 lpcd in stead of 368 lpcd per day.
3. Reduce Birth : death ratio as to become 4.00 by increasing awareness, through campaigns like family planning and by opening family welfare centres.

TABLE 6.5 :
The past, present and the future (predicted) indicator values

Indicator values in Indicators	1961	1971	1981	1991	2001	2011	2021
1. Temperature(max)	44.40	41.10	41.1	46.70	44.70	44.90	45.00
2. Temperature(min)	3.60	1.20	1.30	2.20	1.40	1.20	1.00
3. Land use	0.46	0.551	0.64	0.72	0.81	0.90	0.99
4. Water levels	3.42	2.36	2.14	3.04	1.31	0.78	0.25
5. Population density	4480	5864	7626	9893	11220	12896	14572
6. Birth death ratio	3.01	4.100	3.17	4.64	5.03	5.53	5.04
7. Literacy ratio	0.57	0.585	0.67	0.70	0.81	0.86	0.91
8. Health ratio	0.11	0.526	0.67	0.76	1.12	1.32	1.53
9. Power availability	0.27	0.250	0.53	0.84	1.00	1.00	1.00
10 Occupational structure	0.28	0.255	0.25	0.25	0.23	0.22	0.21
11 Financial receipts	1.06	2.703	8.03	21.34	19.05	23.90	28.76
12 Transportation	55.0	55.00	73.83	143.7	179.3	223.6	267.9
13 Expenditure	10.02	24.97	26.41	92.27	85.19	105.3	123.5

TABLE 6.6 :
Sensitivity analysis (weighing factors)

Basic Indicator	Value	A	B	C	D	E	F	G
		Alternatives						
Environment	0.50	0.90	0.10	0.90	0.90	0.90	0.90	0.90
Climate	0.26	0.26	0.26	0.45	0.10	0.45	0.26	0.26
Terrestrial	0.37	0.37	0.37	0.10	0.45	0.45	0.37	0.37
Aquatic	0.37	0.37	0.37	0.45	0.45	0.10	0.37	0.37
Socio-economy	0.50	0.10	0.90	0.10	0.10	0.90	0.10	0.10
Social	0.60	0.60	0.60	0.60	0.60	0.60	0.10	0.10
Economic	0.40	0.40	0.40	0.40	0.40	0.40	0.90	0.90

TABLE 6.7 :
Modified values according to development options

Indicators	Existing status (1991)	Forecast for 2001 AD	Scenario G1	G2	G3
1. Temperature(max)	46.70	44.70	44.70	44.70	44.70
2. Temperature(min)	2.20	1.40	1.40	1.40	1.40
3. Land use	0.72	0.81	0.65	0.80	0.65
4. Water levels	3.04	1.31	1.92	1.71	1.71
5. Population density	9893	11220	7453	9697	8976
6. Birth death ratio	4.64	5.03	4.01	4.01	5.03
7. Literacy ratio	0.70	0.81	0.98	0.90	0.81
8. Health ratio	0.76	1.12	1.12	1.12	1.34
9. Power availability	0.84	1.00	1.00	1.00	1.00
10.Occupational structure	0.25	0.23	0.27	0.29	0.26
11 Financial receipts	21.34	19.05	20.87	19.05	22.87
12 Transportation	143.7	179.3	215.1	179.3	215.1
13 Expenditure	92.27	85.19	119.1	140.6	147.6

4. Increase literacy by effectively running the evening schools and adult education centers.
5. Enterpreneurship camps to promote self-employment.

ii) Development option G2

1. A provision of minimum 20% of open area around buildings. Plantation of trees on either side of roads or in children parks,stadiums etc.
2. Reduce Birth:death ratio as to become 4.00 by increasing awareness, through campaigns like family planning and by opening family welfare centres.
3. Provision for more opportunities for development of self employment based industries.

iii) Development option G3

1. Increasing the Municipal area by 8 km .
2. Plantation of trees on either side of roads or in parts etc.
3. Increasing Medical Facilities and no. of doctors in the hospitals.
4. Provision for more opportunities for development of self employment based industries.

For each development option appropriate indicator values and figures of monetary resources were introduced. They wished to know which of these has the potential of achieving the best system-state *vis-a-vis* environmental as well as economic criteria. Accordingly the three scenarios were assessed with the aid of CREAM.

The following decision inputs emerge from the analysis:

i) the *as it is* trend is the least desirable; and
ii) G1 is the best of the options whereas G2 and G3 show marginal improvement over the existing trend.

Graphically, the position of the four scenarios with respect to the *ideal* state is presented in Figure 6.3. The scenario G1 is closest to the *ideal* and therefore the most desirable of the ones considered.

7

SUMMARY AND CONCLUSIONS

The study presents formulations and software packages of a system of three new methodologies for environmental impact assessment. The system enables accomplishment of the three key stages of EIA: impact identification, trend analysis/forecasting and impact summation. The system has been developed in an attempt to improve upon existing methodologies and also to plug some of the existing knowledge gaps.

The studies are presented in the following chapters :

CHAPTER I : General Introduction

It gives general introduction to the theme of the treatise.

CHAPTER II : Review of literature and run up to the present treatise

The existing methodologies of environmental impact summation are reviewed in three parts - the commonly used methodologies, less commonly used methodologies, and the emerging ones. In the context of this review, the run up to the present work is put in perspective.

The existing methodologies have some advantages; they also suffer from major shortcomings. Attempts to overcome these shortcomings has led to search of newer techniques and development of newer methods. These aspects are reviewed in detail in the thesis. This review reveals that:

i) there are several less commonly used methodologies or emerging methodologies such as the one based on inter-parameter interactions; none of these have been able to stand the test of extensive field trials; in other words these methodologies are largely confined to paper;
ii) the reasons for this, essentially, are that most of the newer methodologies either require information on the precise nature of inter-parameter relationships (which simply are not available in most cases), or they are computationally or experimentally too cumbersome (and/or unwieldy or costly) to be of much practical utility;
iii) commonly used summation techniques such as the matrix approach have the shortcomings that they are either too simplistic (if used in the two dimensional) form or too cumbersome and costly (if used in three or higher dimensional forms); and
iv) no single *system* of methodologies is available which enables all the three stages of EIA to be accomplished viz a) identification of parameters to be studied b) assessment of their trends and c) impact summation.

In order to overcome some of these shortcomings we have developed a system of three methodologies which may enable all the three stages of EIA to be accomplished. It includes :

i) A formulation and software package for the identification of key parameters out of a large number one invariably encounters during any EIA. It also helps us in arranging the influencing parameters in the order of their importance to generate a hierarchical structure.
ii) A designer software package incorporating the tests and tools needed to process basic data pertaining to typical EIA.
iii) A methodology and software package to integrate the individual environmental impacts for generating net impact scores. This system also enables generation of scenarios and deciding which of the scenarios are environmentally viable.

CHAPTER III : The locale and its environmental indicators used in the present study

In this chapter the study area used for demonstrating the methodologies developed by us, is described. The data and the indicators used in the study are also presented.

The main considerations behind using Roorkee as study area are:

i) its cultural and political ethos, its multi-religion mix, and its distinct layers of socio-economic strata are all representative of a typical Indian city; indeed of all typical Asian cities;
ii) it is not a heavily industrialised city; therefore the impacts of industrialisation do not dominate the city's system but are among the several other contributory factors. In this respect too, the city is representative of a very large number of similar urban systems of Asia;
iii) all three predominant seasons - summer, winter, and monsoon - are witnessed in Roorkee;
iv) eventhough it is a major educational and tourist attraction, the city does not have significant floating population; and
v) basic data of adequate depth and reliability is available for this city albeit in diverse and difficult-to-access sources;

CHAPTER IV : Identification and classification of key parameters and their roles

In this chapter a methodology for distinguishing the more important parameters from the less important ones, developed by us, is described. The methodology aims at identifying key parameters for study in a given EIA situation, thereby helping in reducing time, effort, and cost of EIA.

It is based on the Interpretive Structural Modelling (ISM) and Fuzzy MICMAC (*Matrice d'Impacts Croises - Multiplication Appliqnce a un Classement* or cross impact matrix-multiplication applied to classification) methods, and has the set of formulations shown in Figure 4.1.

When applied to Roorkee, the INTRA analysis reveals that the main factor impacting the environmental system of Roorkee is *population density*, it occupies the most important position among all impacting indicators. The entire system is conditioned to it.

CHAPTER V : Developmental trends and their environmental impacts

In this chapter the software package SMART-ALEC (Statistical Measurements for Assessing Regional Trends And Longterm Environmental Consequences) developed by us to assist in processing information for EIA is described. The package incorporates several statistical tests encompassing deterministic, stochastic, parametric and nonparametric statistics. The use of SMART-ALEC in studying developmental activities and their impacts on environment *vis-a-vis* the city of Roorkee is demonstrated.

Attempts have been made to have the package as user-friendly as possible; the package is capable of execution in two modes - *specific test* and *automatic*. In the specific test mode the user can ask the package to execute only the test he/she desires. In the 'automatic' mode, the package would execute one by one all the tests (if necessary) leaving the user to assess for himself/herself which of the tests lead to significant results.

The package is so designed that the print-outs of the results not only give the numerical values of the various analyses but also gives interpretation of the findings. Further the print-outs are in a form which are directly usable in the preparation of reports.

The study of Roorkee revealed a number of trends, several of which were quantified with the help of SMART-ALEC :

i) Developmental trends

i) During the initial years of development, the urban structure of Roorkee was 'open grained single nuclei' type, which gradually got transformed to 'compact grained multiple nuclei' type. This was accompanied with a high rate of increase in population density.
ii) There has been an overall rise of 485% in population during the last 90 years; the maximum rise occurring in the 1940s and

the minimum rise, 3.2%, during 1901-1911. Regression test indicates statistically significant 'rising trend' ; the Mean Square Successive Difference Test typifies the trend as 'long-term'.

iii) The information on male : female ratio presents surprisingly sharp decline of the order of about 40% during the initial four decades of this century. The data thereafter shows a stabilizing trend, yet the current value (.625) is far less than the national average of 0.927. These results point towards the possibility of a higher female mortality rate.

iv) There is a slow and steady trend of increasing female literacy over the last four decades while the progress in male literacy has been inconsistent. For both sexes the current level of literacy is significantly lower than the national average (62.86% in males and 39.42% in females).

v) Although the number of total workers has increased from 9634 to 20348, the ratio of workers to population has steadily declined (from 0.286 to 0.254).

vi) There is a statistically significant decreasing trend in the instances of death and an increasing trend in the birth : death ratio; an increase of over 100% has been observed during the last four decades.

vii) Medical facilities in Roorkee have received a tremendous boost during the last decade.

viii) The impact of the growth is evidenced by an increase in the municipal receipts and the length of roadways. Similar rising trend is seen in the extent of electrification.

ii) Environmental impacts

i) The maximum ambient temperatures have steadily increased and the minimum ambient temperatures have steadily decreased over the years.

ii) The statistical trend line shows a visible decrease in annual rainfall though the trend is not yet highly significant, being below 90% confidence level.

iii) There is an increase in the noise and air pollution levels. As Roorkee does not have any major industries, the deterioration in the quality of these environmental factors is evidently caused by the vehicular traffic and the din created by human activity in the highly populated areas.

iv) The impact of rapid urbanisation is seen in the changing land use pattern during the years 1961 through to 1991. The percentage of built up area has increased from 45% (in 1961) to 72% (in 1991), causing a 27% decrease in the productive agricultural land of the town and its surroundings.

v) There is a 17% increase in run-off over the last two decades; causing diminished recharging of groundwater.

vi) The water table displays a visibly decreasing trend. The decreasing recharge rate is likely to be due to a combination of these factors: decrease in rainfall during 1975-1991; continuously increasing built-up area; and gradually increasing withdrawal.

vii) There is a significant increase in hardness of water over the years.

viii) The present disposal site for the roughly 200 tones per day garbage as also the town's sewage, is situated upstream of the aquifer serving the town's water supply. There is thus vary strong possibility of the present waste disposal site causing contamination of the entire aquifer thereby adversely affecting the town's water supply.

CHAPTER VI : A new methodology and software package CREAM for impact summation

This chapter presents a methodology to understand the system *as a whole* and describes a software package CREAM (Computer-aided Rapid impact Evaluation And Management) articulated by us that enables user-friendly utilisation of this methodology.

The applicability of the package was demonstrated in generating and evaluating developmental scenarios for the city of Roorkee. Thirteen developmental parameters (identified earlier by INTRA) were used for the study : *temperature (max/min), land use, water levels, population density, birth-death ratio, literacy ratio, health ratio, power availability, occupational structure, financial receipts, transportation,* and *expenditure.* Their values for the past 40-90 years were obtained from archives and used to forecast the scenario in 2001 AD if the past trends persist *as they are.* The weighing factors for the second and third level indicators were then set and sensitivity analysis was performed to identify the indicators likely to play a key role in influencing the system state. The three goals or likely scenarios based on developmental strategies devised by the Municipal Council of the city of Roorkee were also considered. The three scenarios (G1, G2 and G3) were then analysed using CREAM. This led to the following conclusions usable in decision-making :

i) The system state in the last four decades has been gradually shifting away from environmentally compatible zone and by the end of this century it may become environmentally unacceptable.

ii) G1 is the best of the options whereas G2 and G3 show only a marginal improvement over the existing trend.

REFERENCES

Abbasi, S.A.: 1991a, *Environmental Impact of Water Resources Projects in Krishna-Mahanadi-Godavari River Basins,* Discovery Publishing House, New Delhi, xiii+198 pages.

Abbasi, S.A.: 1991b, *Impact of Pulp and Paper effluents on an Estury of Malabar Coast,* Journal of the Institution of Public health Engineers, vol.1991, pp.28-37.

Abbasi, S.A.: 1995a, *ON FUTURES - Selected Technique and Applications,* Discovery Publishing House, New Delhi, 151 pages.

Abbasi, S.A.: 1995b, *Wastewater Treatment Using Aquatic Plants,* Reliance Publications, New Delhi, in press.

Abbasi, S.A.: 1995c, *Urban-Rural Alternative Energy Management,* International Book distributors, Dehradun, in press.

Abbasi, S.A. and Bhatia, K.K.S. : 1993a, *A Environmental Impact of Water Resources Projects in Mahanadi River basin,* vol.9, pp.71-77.

Abbasi, S.A. and Krishna, S.: 1993b, *The New Japanese Pesticide CARTAP(PADAN) - As Safe As Claimed ?,* Ashish Publishing House, New Delhi, xi+152 pages.

Abbasi, S.A., Nipaney, P.C., Soni, R and Arya, D.S. : 1992, *Assesement of Water Quality Creteria for Cobalt, Nickel and Copper vis-a-vis Impact Studies on Freshwater Teleost 'Nuria Denricus',* Journel of the IPHE, vol. 1992(2),pp. 8-18.

Abbasi, S.A. and Nipaney P.C.: 1993, *Modelling and Simulation of Biogas Systems Economics,* Ashish Publishing House, New Delhi, xviii+356 pages

Abbasi, S.A., Nipaney, P.C. and Arya, D.S. : 1994, *Heavy Metals in the Sediments of a river Impacted by Pulp-and-Paper Effulents,* Journel of the IPHE, vol. 1994(2),pp. 18-23.

Abbasi, S.A. and Vinithan, S.V.:1995, *A Delphi for Setting Water and Air Quality Standards Appropriate for Pondicherry*, Centre for pollution Control & Biowaste Energy, pondicherry University (unpublished work).

Abbasi, S.A. etal. : 1995, *Perspectives for Ecology Application - a Forecasting Study, in Futurology - Techniques and Application*, Discovery Publishing House, New Delhi, pp.122-130.

Abonyi, G.: 1980, *Social Assessment Module: Highway Infrastructure Version*, Project Assessment and Evaluation Branch, Department of Regional Economic Expansion.

Abonyi, G.: 1982, *SIAM: Strategic Impact and Assumption - Identification Method for Project, Program, and Policy Planning*, Technological Forecasting and Social Change, vol.22, pp.31-52.

Agrawal, A.: 1995, *Missing the Woods for The Trees*, Down To Earth, vol.4(5), pp.34.

Armstrong, J.S.: 1978, *Long Range Forecasting: from Crystal Ball to Computer*, John Wiley & Sons, NY.

Arya, D.S.: 1991, *Trends of Urbanisation in Roorkee and its Impact on Environment*, M.E. Dissertation, University of Roorkee, Roorkee.

Arya, D.S. and Abbasi, S.A.: *1992, SMART : A New Software Package as Aid in Environmental Management*, Proceedings of ENVIROPRO-'92', Environmental Management Research Association, Malaysia.

Arya, D.S. and Abbasi, S.A.: 1995, *Urbanization and its Environmental Impacts*, Discovery Publishing House, New Delhi, xii+193 pages.

Arya D.S., Joshi, H. and Abbasi, S.A.: 1995, *JESEW-AMUST : A Software Package for Environmental Impact Assessment and Development Planning of Urban Systems*, Journal of Environmental Monitoring and Assessment, communicated.

Arya D.S., Joshi, H. and Abbasi, S.A.: 1994, *Developmental Trends and their Environmental Impact in a Typical Central Indian Town with Special Reference to Roorkee*, Journal of Environmental Monitoring amd Assessment, vol.33, pp.135-150.

Arya D.S., Joshi, H. and Abbasi, S.A.: 1992, *Urbanisation of Roorkee: A Study of Typifying Urban Development in India and its Impacts*, Geographical Review of India, Calcutta, in press.

Austin, L.M. and Burns, J.R.: 1985, *Management Science - An Aid for Management Decision Making*, MacMillan Publishing Company, NewYork.

Associated Industrial Consultants Private Limited (AIL) :1990, Report on EIA Studies for Unit 6 & 7 at Parli Vaijnath District - BEED Maharashtra, Bombay.

Bardossy, A.: 1984, *The Mathematics of Composite Programming, Working Paper*, Tiszadata, Miko, u.1.1012. Budapest, Hungary.

Benarie, M.: 1988, *Delphi-and Delphilike Approaches with Special Regard to Environmental Setting*, Technological Forecasting and Social Change, vol.33, pp.149-158.

Bisset, R.: 1980, *Methods for Environmental Impact Analysis: Recent Trends and Future Prospects*, Journal of Environmental Management, vol.11, pp.1-17.

Black, R.L., Oldham, J.B. and Marcy, W.M.: 1994, *Training KSIM Models from Time Series Data*, Technological Forecasting and Social Change, vol.47(3).

Born, S.M. and Sonzoni, W.C.: 1995, *Integrated Environmental Management: Strengthening the Perspectives*, Environmental Management, vol.19(2), pp.167-183.

Burns, J.R. and Marcey, W.M.: 1979, *Causality: its Characterization in System Dynamics and KSIM Models of Socio-economic Systems*, Technological Forecasting and Social Changes, vol.14, pp.387-398.

Camara, A.S., Ferreira, F.C., Novre, E., and Fialho, J.E.: 1994, *Pictorial Modelling of Dynamic Systems*, System Dynamics Review, vol.10(4).

Chaudhri I.S.: 1971, *Growth and Planning Problem of Roorkee*, PGD Dissertation, Institute of Town Planners (India), New Delhi.

Chen, K.: 1973, *Input-Output Economic Analysis of Environmental Impact*, IEEE Transactions on Systems - Man and Cybernetics, vol.smc-3(6), pp.539-554.

Coates, J.F.: 1976, *The Role of Formal Models in Technology Assessment*, Technological Forecasting and Social Change, vol.9, pp.139-190.

Cocks, K.D. and Waker, B.H.: 1994, *Construction of Sustainability Criteria to Social Perception of Land Use Options*, Land Degradation and Rehabilitations, vol.5(2), pp.143-153.

Colforn, T.: 1994, *The Wildlife/Human Connection: Modernizing Risk Decision*, Environmental Health Perspectives, vol.(102), pp.55-61.

Coppock, R.: 1985, Social Constraints to the Technology Progress, Gower.

Cresser, M. and Edwards, A.:1987, *Acidification of freshwaters, Cambridge University Press, Cambridge.* Centre for Science & Engineering (CSE):1990, State of India'a Environment - A citizen's report (Floods, Flood Plains and Environmental myths), CSE, New Delhi.

Davis, J.C.: 1973. *Statistics and Data Analysis in Geology,* John Willey and Sons, New York.

Davos, C.A.: 1977, *A Priority-tradeoff-scanning Approach to Evaluation in Environmental Management,* Journal of Environmental Management, vol.5, pp.259-273.

Dee, N., Baker, J., Drobny, N., Duke, K. and Fahringer, D.: 1973, *Environmental Evaluation System for Water Resources Planning,* Water Resources Research, vol.9(3), pp.523-535.

District Census Hand Book (DCH) of Saharanpur (Vol.II, Part II-A): (1951), Superintendent of Census Operation Uttar Pradesh, Lucknow.

District Census Hand Book (DCH) of Saharanpur (Vol.X, Part A & B): (1961), Superintendent of Census Operation Uttar Pradesh, Lucknow.

District Census Hand Book (DCH) of Saharanpur (Vol.X, Part A & B): (1971), Superintendent of Census Operation Uttar Pradesh, Lucknow.

District Census Hand Book (DCH) of Saharanpur (Vol.X, Part A & B): (1981), Superintendent of Census Operation Uttar Pradesh, Lucknow.

Doane, D.P.: 1985, *Exploring Statistics for Bussiness and Economics,* Bussiness Publication, Inc. Duperrin, J.C., and Godet, M.: 1973, Methode de Hierarchisation des elements d'un Systeme, Rapport Economique du CEA, 45-51.

Fisher, J., and Davies, G.: 1973, *An Approach to Assessing Environmental Impacts,* Journal of Environmental Management, vol.1, pp.207-227.

Gadgil, M.: 1993, *Biodiversity and India's Degraded Lands,* AMBIO, vol.22(2-3), pp167-172.

Garg, R.K.: 1989, *Impact of Floating Population on the Development of Hardwar,* MURP Dissertation, University of Roorkee, Roorkee. Gibbs, J.P.: 1961, Urban Research Methods, D. Van Nostrand Company INC, New Jersey.

Glasby, G.P.: 1995, *Concept of Sustainable Development: A Meaningful Goal, Science of the Total Environment,* vol.159(1)Jan., pp.67-81.

Grahm, N.E.: 1995, *Simulation of Recent Global Temperature Trends,* Science, vol.267(5198).

Grewal, P.S.: 1987, *Numerical Methods of Statistical Analysis,* Sterling Publishers Pvt. Ltd, New Delhi.

Gupta, R.C.: 1985, *Urban Geography of Delhi-Shahadra,* Bhavana Publication, Delhi.

Heer, J.J. and Hagerty, J.: 1977, *Environmental Assessments and Procedures,* Von Nostrand Reinhold Company.

Indian Meteorological Department (IMD): 1988 IMD Monthly and Average Rainfall Data and Raindays (1901-1950), Part III A (U.P.), IMD, Pune.

Indian Meteorological Department (IMD): 1994 IMD Daily Weather Reports (1951-1994), IMD, Pune.

Jain, R.K.: 1982, *Environmental Conscious Settlement Planning,* A Proc. of All India Conference on Human Settlement, Calcutta.

Jain, R.K.: 1984, *Urbanization and Environmental Impact,* Department of Architecture & Planning (Unpublished work), University of Roorkee, Roorkee.

Jeffery, J.: 1987, *Business Forecasting Methods,* Basil Blackwell, New York.

Joseph, G.V.M. and Glenn, H.G.: 1991, *Statistics for Business and Economics,* Business Publication, Inc.

Kalshian, R.:1995, *Killer Chlorine,* Down To Earth, vol.4(5), pp.29-36.

Kandel, A.: 1986, *Fuzzy Mathematical Techniques with Application,* Addison-Wesley publishing company, Amsterdam.

Kane, J., 1972, *A Primer for a New Cross-Impact Language - KSIM,* Technological Forecasting and Social Change, vol.4, pp.129-142.

Kane, J., Thompson, W. and Vertinsky, I.: 1972, *Health Care Delivery: A Policy Simulator*, Socio-economic Planning Sciences, vol.6, pp.283-293.

Kane, J., Vertinsky, I. and Thompson, W.: 1973, *KSIM: A Methodology for Interactive Resource Policy Simulation*, Water Resources Research, vol.9(1), pp.65-79.

Kumar, A.: 1983, *Time Series Modelling (SA-1)*, National Institute of Hydrology , Roorkee.

Lang, L.: 1994, *Environmental Impact on Hearing: Is Anyone Listening*, Environmental Health Perspectives, vol.102(11).

Lazaro, T.R.: 1979, *Urban Hydrology*, Ann. Arbor Science Publishers INC, Michigan.

Lemons, J.: 1995, *Sustainable Development and Environmental Protection: A Perspective on Current Trends and Future Option for Universities*, Environmental Management, vol.19(2), pp.157-167.

Leontief, W.W.: 1965, *The Structure of U.S. Economy*, Scientific American, vol.212(4), pp.25-35.

Leopold, L.B., Clarke, F.E., Hanshaw, B.B. and Balsley, J.R.: 1971, *A Procedure for Evaluating Environmental Impact*, Geological Survey Circular 645, Government Printing Office, Washington.

Levin, R.I.: 1990, *Statistics for Management*, Prentice Hall of India Pvt. Ltd., New Delhi.

Linstone, H.A.: 1984, *Multiple Perspectives for Decision Making*, North Holland, New York.

Linstone, H.A., Lendaris, G.G., Rogers, S.D., Wakeland, W. and Williams, M.: 1979, *The Use of Structural Modelling for Technology Assessment*, Technological Forecasting and Social Change, vol.14, pp.291-327.

Maiers and Sherief, Y.S.: 1985, *Application of Fuzzy Set-theory*, IEEE Transactions on Systems - Man and Cybernetics, SNC-15(1), pp.175-178.

Makridakis, S., Wheelwright, S.C. and McGee, V.E.: 1983, *Forecasting: Methods and Applications*, John Wiley & Sons Inc.

Meadows, P., and Mizrachi, E.M.: 1976, *Urbanism, Urbanisation and Change, Comparative Prospectus*, Adderson-Westely Publishing Company, New York.

Michener, W.K., Brunt, J.W. and Stafford, S.G. (eds): 1994, *Environmental Information Management and Analysis: Ecosystem to Global Scales*, Taylor and Francis Ltd., London.

Mitra, A.: 1980, *Population and Area of Cities Towns and Urban Agglomeration (1872-1971)*, Jawaharlal Nehru University, Delhi.

Mohapatra, P.K.J.: *Forecasting Based on Cross-impact Analysis*, unpublished work, IIT Kharagpur, India.

Mongkol, P.: 1982, *A Conceptual Development of Quantitative Environmental Impact Assessment Methodology for Decision-makers*, Journal of Environmental Management, vol.14, pp.301-307.

Montgomery, D.R.: 1995, *Input and Output Oriented Approaches to Implementing Ecosystem Management*, Environmental Management, vol.19(2), pp.183-189.

Municipal Board (MB): 1990, MB Nirikshan Tippani , Municipal Board, Roorkee.

Munn, R.E., 1975. *Environment Impact Assessment*, Scope Report-19, John Wiley and Sons, Toronto,

National Institute of Hydrology (NIH): 1988, NIH Workshop on Flood Frequency Analysis, NIH, Roorkee.

National Environmental Ejginaering Research Insipqta (NEERI) :1992, EIA of Reliance Petrochemicals Complex, Hazira, NEERI, Nagpur.

National Environmental Engineering Research Insitute (NEERI) :1992, Rapid EIA of Vijaipur Fertilizer Plants Expansion Project vol 1,NEERI, Nagpur.

National Environmental Engineering Research Insitute (NEERI) :1992, Comprehensive EIA of Visakh Refinary, Visakhapatnam, NEERI, Nagpur.

National Environmental Engineering Research Insitute (NEERI) :1992, Environmental Impact and Risk Assessment of Proposed phase III expansion programme - Hindustan Organic Chemicals Ltd., rasayani, NEERI, Nagpur.

National Environmental Engineering Research Insitute (NEERI) :1993, Rapid EIA of Hindustan Organic Chemicals Limited Cochin, NEERI, Nagpur.

Nevill, H.R.: 1921, *District Gazetteers of the United Provinces of Agra and Oudh (Vol.II) Saharanpur*, Government Press, United Provinces, Lucknow.

Nuruddin,A.A.B., Derus, A.R.B.M. and Ibrahim, S.B. :1987, *Environmental Assesmental Techniques for Tree Harvesting Operations in the Hill Forest of Peninsular*, Malaysia, Asian Environment, pp.11-19.

Rockhoue, K.H.: 1994, *A Decision Analytic Framework for Environmental Analysis and Simulation Modelling*, Environmental Toxicology and Chemistry, vol.13(12).

Saeed, M.Y.: 1987, *Impact of Urbanization on Hydrological Regime in Delhi Region*, M.E. Special Problem, University of Roorkee, Roorkee.

Sawyer, C.N. and McCarthy, L.P.: 1985, *Chemistry for Environmental Engineering*, McGraw-Hill Book Company, Tokyo.

Saxena, J.P., Sushil and Vrat, P.: 1990a, *Fuzzy Interpretive Structural Modelling Applied to Energy Conservation*, Socio-Economic Planning & Sciences.

Saxena, J.P., Sushil and Vrat, P.: 1990b, *Impact of Indirect Relationship in Classification of Variables - a MICMAC Analysis for Energy Conservation*, System research, vol.7, pp.245-253.

Saxena, J.P.and Vrat, P.: 1990c, *Linkages of Key Elements in Fuzzy Programme Planning*, System Research, vol.7, pp.147-158.

Saxena, J.P., Sushil and Vrat, P.: 1992, *Scenario Building: A Critical Study of Energy Conservation in the Indian Cement Industry*, Technological Forecasting and Social Changes, vol.41, pp.121-146.

Soil Conservation Services (SCS) National Engineering handbook Sec(4) Hydrology. 1972, U.S. Department of Agriculture, Washington.

Seth, S.M. and Goel, N.K.: 1985, *Frequency Analysis UM-2*, National Institute of Hydrology, Roorkee.

Setin, S. and Chavez, D.: 1995, *Developing a Collaborative Model for Environmental Planning and Management*, Environmental Management, vol.19(I), pp.189-197.

Shopley, J.B. and Fuggle. R.F.: 1984, *A Comprehensive Review of Current Environmental Impact Assessment - Methods and Techniques*, Journal of Environmental Management, vol.18, pp.25-47.

Sondheim, M.W.: 1978, *A Comprehensive Methodology for Assessing Environmental Impact*, Journal of Environmental Management, vol.6, pp.27-42.

Soni, B. and Mishra, G.C.: 1986, *Soil Water Accounting Using SCS Hydrological Soil Classification*, Report CS-15, National Institute of Hydrology, Roorkee.

Sundaresan, B.B.: 1989, *EIA of SPIC fine chemicals Karaikal,* Vimta Industrial consultants(P) Ltd., Secundrabad.

Lawson, T.L.: 1986, 'Deforestation and Induced Changes in Meso/micro Climate', in: Lal, R., Sanchez, P.A. and Cummings(Jr), R.W. (eds), *Land Clearing and Development in the Tropics,* A.A. Balkuma publisher, Netherlands, pp.195-202.

UNESCO: 1984, *Hydro Environmental Indices: A Review and Evaluation of their Use in the Assessment of the Environmental Impacts of Water Projects,* IHP-II, Project A 3.2, Peris.

UNESCO: 1988, *Training Guidance for the Integrated Environmental Evaluation of Water Resources Development Projects,* Peris.

University of Roorkee (UOR): 1967, UOR Souvenir - 120 Years of Progress 1847-1967, Director Technical Publication, University of Roorkee, Roorkee.

University of Roorkee: 1990, UOR Information Bulletin 1990, University of Roorkee, Roorkee..

Unlu, K.: 1994, *Assessing Risk of Ground Water Pollution from Land-disposed Wastes,* Journal of Environmental Engineering, vol.120(6), pp.1578-98.

UP Jal Nigam: 1989, Roorkee Water Supply Scheme for 1989-1990 Immediate Relief, Uttar Pradesh Jal Nigam Roorkee,Uttar Pradesh.

Vishwamitter and Jain R.K.: *Science and Sense of Settlement. Transportation and Urban Structures,* Unpublished work, Department of Architecture and Planning, University of Roorkee, Roorkee.

Vizaykumar, K. and Mohapatra, P.K.J.: 1989a, *An Approach to Environmental Impact Assessment by Using Cross Impact Simulation,* Environmental and Planning A, vol.2, pp.830-837.

Vizaykumar, K. and Mohapatra, P.K.J.: 1989b, *A Dynamic Simulation Model for Environmental Impact Analysis,* System Dynamics, pp.45-61.

Vizaykumar, K. and Mohapatra, P.K.J.: 1989c, An *Interpretive Structural Model of Environmental Impacts of Coal Field,* Journal of Environmental Systems, vol.19(1), pp.71-93.

WaLL, F.: 1986. *Statistical Data Analysis Handbook*, McGraw-Hill Book Company, New York.

Warfield, J.N.: 1977, *Societal Systems: Planning, Policy and Complexity*, Wiley, New York.

Watson, R.H.: 1978, *Interpretive Structural Modelling - A Useful Tool for Technology Assessment*, Technological Forecasting and Social Changes, vol.11, pp.165-185.

Zadeh, L.A.: 1965, *Fuzzy Sets*, Information and Control, vol.8, pp.338-353.

●●●